MINDFULNESS

A Teenager's Guide to Managing Stress and Life Decisions

By Rhonda Duffaut, PhD, RYT

Illustrations by Jersey Benjamin

ISBN: 978-1-64184-418-5 (paperback)

Loving-Kindness Meditation

May you be safe,
May you be healthy,
May you be at ease.

Disclaimer:

CONTENTS

FOREWORD

It was 9th grade when I picked up my first book on Yoga. I'm not sure what inspired me to do so other than a desire to understand human nature. In the science of Yoga, I discovered an exquisite map of consciousness, a guide to "me." I devoured books by Ram Dass, including *Be Here Now*, *Grist for the Mill* and *Journey of Awakening*. I was even lucky enough to find a practice video at the local library. (This was 1981.) Students in leotards wearing lots of make-up in a kitschy scene of fake flowers and bridges giggled their way through poses. Awkwardly practicing along in my basement, I remember thinking, "*this is weird*." But it also drew me in. I felt better. More at ease. More myself. So I worked with the weirdness, and it became more familiar and more comfortable over time. It is now woven into my daily life and has been for four decades. As a yoga therapist and teacher trainer of yoga for children, I can help share this life-affirming practice that was so beneficial to me at a young age.

Dr. Duffaut, too, shares a passion for translating yoga into an approachable practice for young people. Besides her many other credentials, she was a student of our training. I got to see firsthand her heart for the practice of yoga and her enthusiasm for how it can help youth. She also has the discernment of a scientist and decades of both academic study and personal yoga practice. To that, she has added careful listening to her teenage yoga students. This book is the result.

School teaches you how to understand and manage the world around you. There are no classes on how to understand and manage the world within you. And yet, you are expected to become an adult and do just that. Also, the transition you are now in from childhood to adulthood is vague and drawn out. Traditional rituals and rites of passage have fallen away. Adolescence can feel like you've landed in a foreign land with no map or guidebook.

You are holding in your hands such a guide. This is a map to the workings of your own mind. Dr. Duffaut has laid out for you simple yet powerful practices to help you live your best life. It's a guide for growing into adulthood and through life with ease, joy, and purpose. That may feel a long way off for you right now. But if you take these teachings to heart and apply some effort, you'll have more of a sense of yourself and where you're headed in life. That just feels good. And you are in good hands with Dr. Duffaut as she has worked with young people like you for many years. When I talk with the teenagers in the yoga classes I teach, I hear from them that they often feel adults (especially their parents) just don't "get" them. Well, Dr. Duffaut gets you. And she's got your back as she guides you through the practice of Yoga. It will teach you, as she says in this book, "how to be yourself, be with yourself, and be in peace with yourself."

Mira Binzen, C-IAYT, E-RYT 500, RCYT
Co-Founder, Global Family Yoga

INTRODUCTION

"You are all attached to your mats. Just do," my teacher in India told the class as we scrambled back to "our" mats in order to try the pose.[1] First of all, the mats belonged to the institute. Second, they all looked the same. Although finding that particular one among a hundred lying side by side posed challenging, we didn't hesitate to try. Why? The teacher wasn't interested in which mat we used or whether we even used a mat.

Humans form attachments to objects, people, and places. We develop likes and dislikes, and even though these might change as our environment changes (i.e., transferring schools or cities), we still become attached. Sometimes we even form habits that aren't healthy for us. The kind of attachments you have or the lack of attachments cause stress. You might have experienced worry, heightened emotions, or tension in your body as a reaction to stress. The more awareness of ourselves we have, the better we will be able to determine the types of connections we form and manage our reactions. Patanjali, an Indian philosopher who lived in the second century BCE, claimed that we gain more awareness when we practice the mindfulness of yoga.

Yoga is union. It literally means connecting or melding together. In practicing yoga, you bring yourself into the present moment, experiencing yourself in that moment. Totally present, you don't think about how much more time you have or how much more you have to do. On the other hand, when you are stressed, emotions set off anxious thoughts and physical tension that separate you from experiencing the moment you are in. It's the difference between reading a chapter in a book for school, all along counting the pages left to read, and reading that same chapter focused on the content in front of you so that the wait for the end seems to disappear.

Patanjali, who will be our guide through this book, defines yoga in his book, *Yoga Sutras*, as the progressive quieting of the mind's turbulence.[2] The mindfulness of yoga will sometimes look like you aren't doing anything, like when you meditate or talk to your friends. Other times, it will be a physically active practice. Unlike other activities, you don't need any special equipment to do yoga—just you.

I wrote this book because many adult or children's classes are offered, but few are targeted to teenagers' developing bodies and minds. On top of that, many high school students are too busy to commit to a weekly class, or others practice yoga on their own to avoid being judged. And yet, the skill we want to learn—mindfulness both on and off the mat—is something everyone can achieve.

You can use this guide in several ways. The structure allows you to read and contemplate about what yoga is and does for you when you practice. The boxes on the sides offer shortened explanations and practices, like a brief takeaway, that you can think about and do anywhere. The later chapters guide you through shifting your attitudes, mentally and physically, with physical sequences. Lastly, you will have space to journal at the end of each chapter to tie your experience together.

SECTION I
THEORY

I.1 Yoga and Teens: Making More Decisions on Your Own

I started yoga as an adult to help recover from an injury. What I discovered after the first class is that it not only helped my physical body feel stronger and more supple, but it gave me peace of mind to make some tough decisions about my future. I wish someone had introduced me to yoga when I was a teenager, when I was beginning to make more and more decisions for myself.

When you make a choice *for* something, you simultaneously choose *against* something else. This can set off feelings of stress and anxiety that will affect both mind and body in your attempt to make the "right" decision. The mindfulness practices of yoga help relieve anxious feelings as you learn to trust yourself. I am not claiming that yoga will guide you to the "right" decision. Nevertheless, it will give you the tools to seek decisions about friends, school, behavior, and the future in order to better navigate your life.

The Context

What we see and hear about yoga today comes from the writings of Patanjali, who lived almost 2,000 years ago. He wrote 196 *sutras*—short statements or "words of wisdom"—for the first time categorizing classical yoga, also called Raja Yoga (royal yoga). These words of wisdom, which were previously passed along orally as stories in songs, he titled *Yoga Sutras*. No one knows for sure whether he was one person or, as was the practice back then, a group of people. This might seem strange to us who seek followers on social media to "like" us as individuals. However, in Patanjali's time, people believed knowledge passed down couldn't and shouldn't be attributed to any *one* person.

The tradition comes from India, which has a very different culture from our Western one. The language is Sanskrit, one of the oldest, if not *the* oldest, languages. Any time we translate the writings about yoga in our language, we interpret them. This is the case with any translation, but it's even more challenging for a language like Sanskrit, in which one word can have up to six definitions that might change depending on its relationship to other words. The language itself emphasizes the importance of relationships.

The philosophy and religion of this time were based on an immortal non-judging entity, a supreme being.[3] While people's relationship to this divinity transformed as different cultures moved into India, this idea of non-judgment remained constant. To become close to divinity meant not judging others, not judging yourself.

Interaction was another key element of Indian culture. Historically, rituals of interaction, in which one item is exchanged for another item of equal value, were a way to support one's family in India. This interaction maintained the health of family members. Exchange, in addition to the belief in an immortal entity that unifies all life, helped to foster acceptance of one's circumstances. Acceptance of one's situation was important since social class, often defined by one's last name, determined a person's life (home, work, lifestyle).

Exchange and Consequence

While ancient and modern Indian culture is very different from modern Western culture, two ideas are familiar to us and form the basis of yoga.

- **The ritual of exchange—you give and will receive of comparable value**
- **The idea of karma—your actions have consequences to *you***

Patanjali incorporates these ideas throughout the *Sutras* and impresses upon us that yoga is interaction. Sometimes that interaction is active—doing with others, with oneself, and with objects. Other times it appears passive because the doing is internal. We do not always experience interaction as an even exchange, but seeing your connection to your environment as exchanges that you navigate can help you better manage those experiences.

This is how exchange works: The value you take away directly relates to the effort you put in, regardless of the outcome. For example, if you study for a test and do well, you affirm your knowledge of the material. If you don't study and do well, you confirm that you already have a grasp of the material. If you study and do poorly, you realize you still did not understand, and that's valuable knowledge. Notice how I didn't even mention grades because maybe you learn other lessons about unfairness that will aid you in your next interaction. However, the smoother the exchange goes, the better you feel.

Karma works like this: What you do ultimately comes back to you, physically and emotionally. You hit your brother. He hits you back or tells on you. You throw a can in the lake. Yours won't kill the fish, but others see your can and throw theirs in. Eventually, the lake is full of garbage, and you can no longer swim in it. You smile at the bus driver, and she offers you a friendly greeting. You lie about attending a party, and the consequence might not be immediate, but the mental and emotional strain persists.

"How much more interaction can I have?" you ask. "I am constantly connected to friends and family with my cell phone."

Yes, you can share anything instantaneously. But are you in this particular moment of interaction? Did you quickly type a response while you were doing your homework or talking to someone else?

The types of interactions you have affect you, and some of your behaviors are better for you than others. For example, loyalty to friends is a good quality. But what if a friend asks you to shoplift? According to Patanjali, some behavior is toxic, meaning it lingers with you afterward and shadows future interactions. Questions you might ask yourself as you act with more personal responsibility are "How does my behavior affect me? How does it affect others?"

Presence

"I live in the moment! When I'm with my friends, we do crazy things. I don't think about the future," you say. It is possible to be physically present and not mentally present. That's why I direct students to bring their mind into their body to be where their body is. You can do this by focusing on your breath. Your breath is a gauge. If you breathe smoothly, you are at ease. You might find yourself taking a deep breath with a long exhalation before a presentation or a big test. Doing so can slow down your heart rate and calm your nervous system.

If you breathe erratically, holding your breath or puffing through your mouth, it speeds up your heart because you work harder to draw in oxygen. Your nervous system also has to work harder because you send it mixed signals.

Doing yoga is more than learning to **move your body attentively.** When you fill your mind with the present moment, you **practice being mindful**. As you read before, yoga philosophy acknowledges that you are in this world with other beings and objects. Your interactions with these will determine the struggles you have along the way (consequences and exchange). The decisions you make and your attitudes become **mindfulness in action**. This means you steer it with the decisions you make as you pay attention to your attitude on and off the mat.

> Mindfulness Practice
>
> Breath Focus: With your eyes closed or open, draw your attention to your breath. Take a deep breath in through your nose and breathe deeply out through your mouth. On your next breath, close your mouth, slow down your exhalation through your nose so that it's longer than your inhalation. Breathe through your nose 3-5 times and take a moment to examine how you feel.

The yoga we Westerners are most familiar with consists of physical postures practiced on a mat. However, yoga poses are not the only part of yoga that helps you pay attention. Even before you step on the mat, it is assumed that you are preparing yourself with smooth interactions and healthy decisions. This frees you to better focus in and on the poses, strengthening your body and mind, to sit in a silent practice of meditation. Patanjali's practice begins in everyday life with mental and physical preparation off the mat.

Thus, yoga speaks to all humanity, and embraces all humanity, as fully capable of participating because it is in *doing* that yoga happens. Mindfulness off the mat is as significant as on the mat. It is often easier to be attentive in your own space on your mat in a relatively silent room, where mostly everyone there has a similar mindset. Everyone is doing on the mat that they have claimed. The poses on the mat bring your attitudes into focus because you experience them physically.

What about outside of class, off the mat? How are you supposed to show kindness towards an annoying sibling or aggravating parent or hurtful bully? How does touching your toes help you to see the relevance of honesty? By putting mindfulness into action in your daily life, you develop attitudes that carry you into life so you can better manage the stressors inside and out.

1.2. Why Yoga for You: Diving In

We are a part of nature and are naturally complex. In the ocean, waves continually break on the shore, but they also develop far out from the shore when the wind whips up, creating white caps. Thus, on the surface, the water is turbulent even as it ebbs and flows. Yes, some riptides and currents pull and push, and can be deadly. The deeper down you go, however, the quieter and more methodically life moves, and it's as if you connect to the universe.

Like the ocean, our minds are turbulent. On the surface, we receive information and sensory input; below the surface, thoughts, emotions, and memories swirl around. The universe of your body and mind is fathomless and infinite, layered, and complex. It still holds so many secrets. And yet, if we give it a chance, we too can experience connection with the universe of our body and mind, as well as with our external universe.

Your brain is still developing. From ages 10 to 24, you experience bursts of growth neurologically, physically, emotionally, intellectually, and socially; this constitutes adolescence. The teenage years, the phase between childhood and adulthood, are right in the middle, between the ages of 13 to 19. And yet, the rational part of an adolescent brain is not fully developed until around age 25.

A University of Rochester study has found that teen brains work differently from adult brains because a teen's prefrontal cortex is still forming.[4] Adults think with the prefrontal cortex, the brain's rational center, located behind the forehead. This part of the brain responds with reason and considers long-term consequences. Teens think more with the amygdala, the emotional center of the brain, which sits in the middle of the lobes.

In a teen's brain, the connections between the emotional part of the brain and the decision-making part are still growing, and often at different rates. Emotional input might overpower thought so that you don't take in as much information.[5] For this reason, developing connections is important. Connections between the decision-making area and the emotional area of your brain and to your body, connections with your thoughts and feelings, connections with others and the external world you live in. As you quiet your mind from distractions, you perceive those connections better.

Yoga creates this linking experience. As Patanjali writes, "When we **progressively** steady the mind's movements, we rest in ourselves with ease."[6] You check in with yourself, just as you would with a good friend. And just as you would with a good friend, you try to be present and listen. You might get distracted, but you draw your focus back. Your **mind fills** with what is around you. You are **mindful**.

Creativity

You experience the effect of yoga during the practice. So you can't simply read about it or watch it being done. Your state of mind, your attitude, changes as you progressively do. It's not surprising that the new term for "enlightened" is "woke." You are literally awake to the moment and perceive the world with your five senses: touch, sight, hearing, taste, and smell. You are in that moment.

The process of doing cultivates creativity by expanding you physically and mentally. If you focus on what you are doing, you are forced to slow down both physically and mentally, thereby allowing mental space to explore. When I taught English, one of my favorite writing exercises was descriptive writing because you report what you experience with your five senses. What appears to be a mere assignment turns into a creative practice.

Your mind stretches to accommodate the sensations and beyond when you do the physical practice of yoga poses, stretching your body. When you envision touching your toes, for instance, even if you can't reach them, your imagination extends to the possibility. You visualize it, feel it, and your brain sends messages to the nerve endings to wake them up. Pressing your fingers down becomes an act of pressing, with which your mind is fully engaged so that connections become apparent. For instance, how does pressing your thumb affect your arm, shoulder, back, hip, or leg?

> **Mindfulness Practice**
>
> Visualize a place you enjoy in detail. Aside from how it looks, how does it smell, feel, sound, and taste? Use your five senses in your visualization.

From the time you awake, you filter sensory impulses from outside yourself (light, sounds, smells, tastes, sensations), and you manage sensations within yourself (hunger, emotions, sore muscles). Some of these arise biologically, like hunger or sore muscles. Others arise from the thoughts or feelings of your mind (pleasure, anxiety). You open your eyes and see the sun. Seeing the sun, you think about school. Thinking about school sets off feelings of pleasure or displeasure. Or you feel good until you see something on social media that causes you displeasure, which sets off an array of biological sensations. This up and down, push and pull, continue throughout your day.

1.3. Obstacles: Breaking Through

Many things interfere with our ability to be attentive. Every stage of life brings challenges, but teens struggle to filter input that seems to come from every angle—self, friends, family, teachers, work, strangers, reading, streaming. Patanjali recognized that sometimes our inner steering guide breaks down, and we begin to make unhealthy choices.[7] When we are in any of these states, we can't perceive what is going on and lose the desire to figure it out. You might have experienced any one of these:

Obstacles

- Illness
- Negative self-talk
- Doubt
- Impatience
- Lethargy
- Stress
- Overconfidence/Lack of confidence
- Lack of stamina
- Lapsing into self-destructive behavior

- **Illness: You don't want to do much of anything**. When you are in a weakened physical condition from a cold or the flu to a broken leg or on your monthly cycle, you view the world through discomfort. You feel both emotionally and physically sensitive and might react defensively.
- **Negative self-talk: When you think you aren't good enough, you limit yourself.** Talking down to yourself makes you see yourself negatively and inhibits how you interact with friends or in class.
- **Doubt: When you question your abilities, you might not even try.** By focusing on what you cannot do well, you forget what you can do well. Our brains naturally seek out potential threats to protect us. Based on those threats, we attack, flee, or freeze. If we only think about what might go wrong, we react to something, instead of interacting.
- **Impatience: Impulsiveness results in poor decisions.** Quick decisions can lead to misunderstandings and mistakes. You have a lot going on: school, friendships, family, future goals. You are just getting going and want things to happen *now*. But quick actions can cause harm.
- **Lethargy: Lack of movement results in gradual mental dullness and emotional despair.** You get tired of the demands placed on you. Your body is growing, and you need your sleep. Staying in bed or lying on the couch all day sounds great, but your body and mind were built to move. When you isolate yourself, it becomes more difficult to step back in.

- **Stress: Tension contributes to physical discomfort and, potentially, any of the first five obstacles.** Not being able to manage all your responsibilities generates stress because things are unfinished. The physical effects of stress are similar to the fight/flight response that prepares you for action, which wears you down.
- **Overconfidence/Lack of confidence: Anxiety can arise with a loss of control**. Some people overestimate what they bring to an exchange, and others underestimate themselves. Both are equally problematic because they force you to pretend to be someone you aren't. You might not even realize you are doing this, but it becomes exhausting. The behavior leads you instead of you managing it. You might begin to feel a loss of control.
- **Lack of stamina: It's possible to feel discouraged when you become depleted mentally, physically, and emotionally.** If you can't keep up, you might give in or discontinue an activity. You give in to peer pressure or give up an activity you enjoy because you don't have the mental willpower, the physical strength, or the emotional peace to challenge it.
- **Self-destructive behavior: You lapse into behavior that undermines you.** This is the extreme version of any of the obstacles. Consciously or unconsciously, you begin to harm yourself through your actions.

Any one of these affects your connection between you and the universe. Sometimes you can overcome an obstacle on your own. For example, I try not to listen to negative thoughts when I'm sick because I'm fairly sure that I will think or feel differently about things when I am better. When my children have an important day, I encourage them to leave the house earlier to give themselves more time so as not to become impatient or anxious.

Other times, you will need help to overcome an obstacle. Talking to parents,

Mindfulness Practice
Jyana Mudra

Open your hands: palms facing up, fingers stretching out. Bring your thumb and index finger to touch lightly and draw your others fingers together. Focus your attention on the touch of your two fingers and notice how it changes when your mind drifts. Do this for 1 minute.

Mudras are said to direct the energy in your body. When you make the hand gestures, you do feel your muscles working after holding it awhile. They make you more aware of your hands and your arms and also how things shift. This particular mudra is for concentration and memory.

friends, or a professional can help. Checking in with yourself is equally important to determine this.

If you have time, hop on the mat for some physical poses. If that's not suitable, do a hand mudra (gesture for your hands) that will draw you back to yourself in the moment. If you can't do that, practice shifting your attitude off the mat (in Section II).

I.4. Patterns: Inscribing Your Life

When you pay attention, you also become aware of your physical and mental patterns. From the moment you are born, your life experiences become inscribed in and on you like tattoos—impressions and habits begin to form. If you burn your hand on something hot, you learn to avoid heat that will hurt. You will go to great lengths to avoid a hot surface. By contrast, if you experience something comforting or pleasurable, you will desire this and go to great lengths to obtain it.

> Impressions and habits begin to form the moment you are born.

You might think I am referring to mere objects, but your body reacts on a cellular level. Your brain is not the only part of you that records your life. A new study reveals that cells in your body remember experiences from early life.[8] Something pleasing is embraced, and you relax (i.e., when you listen to music you like or when you receive a hug). By contrast, something unpleasant is rejected, and you tense up. When you eat something extremely distasteful, your entire body contracts in to spit it out. Likewise, when you find yourself in an uncomfortable situation, your body tenses in preparation for action.

This happens so much that over time, your body begins to shape itself around these experiences. If you ball your hands into fists whenever you are angry, nervous, or scared—and are often in these states—it will get to a point where you start to unconsciously form fists, tensing your arm muscles most of the day. Depending on your physical activity, you might have strong but tight muscles on one side of your body to help you throw or run or kick or dance.

It's not just physical activity that shapes your body. Inactivity or holding yourself in one position repeatedly forms your body as well. Just at the moment when you are feeling more confident and want to stretch your wings of independence, you are forced to spend up to seven hours a day with school. Virtual learning requires you to sit even more in place in order to listen or see the screen. After school, there is more work to be done, which probably entails sitting or standing. Less emphasis is placed on stretching the body in different directions, even though you are asked to stretch your mind with knowledge and methods.

Like most natural beings, we extend towards the sun, energy, and vibrancy. But most of us spend our days with our energy directed downwards towards desks, work, and phones. We now communicate with others by looking downwards at them on devices rather than more or less eye-to-eye.

If you sit slouched for long hours, you will begin to experience shortness in your core muscles that pull the top of your spine forward in a downward direction. This postural asymmetry (uneven posture) affects respiration and circulation around the heart. Further, arm and leg muscles shorten, not just from sitting but also from repetitive movements. You might walk up and down stairs, but you do the same amount in the same directions. It keeps you moving, but your body accommodates itself to the movements.

Additionally, bones begin to grow longer at a faster rate than muscles, resulting in shortened muscles and inflexibility around 13 or 14 years of age. This is the time that teens find it difficult to touch the floor by bending forward. You might be surprised at how inflexible you have become because an action, such as bending down with legs straight, grows uncomfortable to perform, and so you avoid it. Thus, you don't notice this change until you stretch.

We think of yoga poses as somewhat bizarre positions into which we have to force our bodies. However, the muscular actions of yoga are actions our body does—stretching, flexing, squeezing, expanding—all the while promoting bone growth and regulating hormones. What we consider to be unusual physical postures of yoga are actually muscle actions and joint positions, for which our bodies are designed. When I had a class do Standing Big Toe Pose (lifting one leg straight in front by holding that foot) with one foot on the wall, one student said it reminded her of how she flushes public toilets with her foot. She demonstrated how she normally lifts one leg to push the lever. This action was very similar to the yoga pose, minus the attention and alignment. Practicing the poses will help maintain strength and suppleness.

We all have tight muscles or physical imbalances and struggle with them throughout life. Even the stress that contributes to tightness and imbalance can benefit us by motivating us into action. However, the sedentary nature of our lives compounds the effect this stress

> Diamonds are dull when found in nature. It is in the cutting and polishing that they shine. Doing yoga sharpens and polishes you so that you shine.

has. Our minds play an important role in enhancing or depleting these, and the practice of yoga can help both the body and the mind.

1.5. The Mirror: Seeing Yourself

Patanjali writes his *sutras* as one-sentence statements, sharing knowledge but also allowing the reader to interpret the meaning in his/her life. This is an old tradition in India. The priests (Brahmins) transmitted ideas symbolically, allowing the receiver to decode them by contemplating them. Imagine receiving an assignment with no description of how to do it. You would have to figure it out yourself. This is similar to our tradition of fables or fairy tales, in which animals and situations, like forests and rivers, represent life experiences.

Once again, we see the connection of exchange. Patanjali establishes an *exchange* between himself and the reader (you read and interpret his writings) but also between you and you (by figuring out what the writings mean, you learn more about yourself). He also describes the consequence to you: doing this will affect you, as with *karma*. For example, if you repeat a word to yourself, you will feel its effect on you, so choose your word with this in mind.

Although his sentences are brief, they thread together an idea. The word *sutra* means "thread," and Patanjali threads together these brief statements with this underlining idea of a state of mind clear of distractions so that you reflect back to you. He uses the image of reflection; if the body is quiet and balanced, the mind becomes quiet and balanced. And a quieted mind can reflect what it perceives clearly, like a mirror or a still lake.[9] If the mirror is foggy or dirty, the reflection is warped, and the information your body and mind receive is faulty because it's incomplete. If the lake is turbulent, like the ocean, what's underneath appears distorted.

What is one of the first things you do when your bathroom mirror is fogged up? You wipe it to clear a section to see yourself. The mirror Patanjali writes about is within you. You use your body and mind to see (perceive) yourself instead of only looking externally for answers.

Since all your mental and physical experiences make you who you are, you reflect what you do, think, and feel. As you move into your teen years, you grow more self-conscious—gradually developing a sense of self in comparison to others around you. When your environment expands, your reflecting surface expands. The internet enables you to be aware of so much in the world. Social media allows you to project the image of yourself you desire at any given time.

You begin to notice that you can steer other people's views by developing a persona and projecting an image of yourself that fits you better in a specific situation. You assume certain labels or looks to orientate yourself. You are a daughter, a son, a student, an athlete, a sibling, a friend, body-positive, thin, a person of color, white, physically girl or boy. These labels and looks define you and give you meaning. But like putting on a particular shirt, you are more one than the other in certain situations. You even try to emphasize your physical attributes over others, wearing looser or tighter clothes.

Like selfies, you project an image, often staged. Sometimes they can get jumbled, or you become pigeonholed in an identity even though you think you are constantly fluctuating. You mirror your friends by using the same expressions, wearing similar outfits, behaving similarly. You feel confident when surrounded by likeminded people. But then you see someone online that makes you question that. You thought you stood out with your behavior but see on YouTube that someone else does the same thing. Or maybe you thought you were the best until you saw that someone does it better. When you reevaluate yourself compared to others instead of checking in with yourself, you become distracted. You lash out at your parents because you don't want to only be seen as the dutiful son or daughter. You feel betrayed because your friend has started dating and doesn't have as much time for you.

This identity ends up confining you at the same time it defines you. It connects you to a certain group and distances you from others. Ultimately, these labels distance you from yourself because they don't embody all of you. You are all those identities, and more. Your identity is constantly changing as you are exposed to new ideas, experiences, and images.

Mindfulness Practice
Om Mantra

Sit comfortably with your hands resting on your legs. Inhale gently and exhale with a lengthy Om or hum. Do this 3 times out loud. Then do this 3 times silently.

The word Om (or Aum) is difficult to define. Rhyming with "dome," it is a combination of three sounds and vibrations: Aaa, Uuu, Mmm. It is said to include the universe since each sound corresponds to past (A), present (U), and future (M). When you repeat this sound, you link time, link to the sound of your voice, link to your body with vibrations, and link to sensations of your muscles creating those sounds. If you'd rather, simply hum so you have the benefit of sound, vibration, and sensation of your body.

Comparing yourself to others is like trying to see through a grimy mirror. By contrast, when you interact with others, you act in relation to another. Acting in relation to another is different than gaining value from another. Whereas comparison is valued interaction (i.e., one is better than the other), relational interaction is more objective (i.e., each gain from the other). Clarity helps to "see" what that relation is.

I.6. The Practice: Keeping Your Mirror Sparkling

Now, what if you could wipe down the mirror to tune in to yourself, quieting the noise for a moment? This means taking out your earbuds for a while or putting down your phone in order to be with yourself or others. It can be a scary prospect to be without all the noise and images that prop you up but also fog your true reflection of that moment. The yoga mat represents a defined space in which to practice this. Out in your boundless life, it's more difficult to form those demarcations (visible boundaries). The practice of mindfulness can create the space and time of presence as if you were on the mat.

Your days are filling up with school, activities, time with friends and family, obligations, and work. When do you have time to step onto a mat and do some physical poses? You don't only have to strike a pose to practice the yoga of Patanjali.

Quieting the noise (cleaning the mirror) begins when you set your mind on one thing. When you are mind-full—when your mind is full of one thing—you truly connect with it. According to Patanjali, you can do this by focusing your attention on one thing—an idea, an action, a word, a physical thing.[10] This is what you have been doing with the mindfulness practices in this manual. When you focus on what you are eating, for example, you notice the flavors, colors, and shapes. Instead of absently eating, you have an experience of eating and all that it brings. Similarly, when you pay attention to what you are doing, you experience it with your five senses—connecting you in that moment.

> It is your intent, your effort, and the enjoyment you bring to life that embodies yoga. Adolescence is a stage in life where intent, effort, and enjoyment grow dim in the face of expectations. You are closer to your passions now than you will be as an adult. Remind yourself by practicing.

How is this different from being absorbed or engrossed in an activity, like social media or streaming? While social media connects you to friends and watching shows connects you to some of your senses, these activities done inattentively create more noise. This is the opposite of "mindful." It's not to say that these are merely mindless activities. You can learn from social media. You can check in with friends with social networking. It is your attitude and intention that differentiates it.

SECTION II
PRACTICE

II.1. Mindfulness in Action: Yamas and Niyamas

You've been reading how and why to practice mindfulness, but what does all this have to do with yoga? To recap, yoga connects you to yourself, others, and the world in general. How does it do this? It gives you a space to be with yourself in the present moment so you can better "see" yourself. Do you have to do the poses to experience the benefits of mindfulness? No.

This is fabulous news because you might not have time for a yoga class. For Patanjali, mindfulness in action occurs *off* the mat as well as *on* the mat. Yoga on the mat does help to focus your attention on your body, and in this way, better helps you experience the connection to yourself.

Patanjali offers several ways to "do" yoga. He maps this out in his eightfold path of yoga. A list of the practices makes it look like one step follows the other to reach a goal. But as we established in the previous chapters, concentration and meditation and breath are equally helpful in bringing you into sync with yourself. Creating a strong body and stabilizing your breath, for example, will help with the other limbs of concentration and meditation because they cultivate ease. He uses the word limb (anga), and like a tree, all the practices link together.

The Eight-Limb Path includes:

- Yama (social attitudes)
- Niyama (individual attitudes)
- Asana (physical postures)
- Pranayama (breath)
- Pratyahara (inward direction of the senses)
- Dharana (concentration)
- Dhyana (meditation)
- Samadhi (self-awareness)

You can do the physical practice of yoga on the mat without the others, but then it is fitness, not mindfulness. Like climbing a tree, you could jump to the highest branch, scraping yourself through the struggle. Or you could start at a closer branch and make your way more smoothly with less effort. Similarly, including the yamas (social attitudes) and niyamas (individual attitudes) guides your physical practice and cultivates a similar ease of mind and body to strive for the other limbs.

The first two limbs (yamas and niyamas) act as your framework. They provide a moral guide for your identity. These principles are not a law or command to be internalized from outside yourself. Rather, they are steps a yoga student can take to gain perspective and clean that incomplete reflection. They are attitudes that, once embraced, inform your actions. The first group, yamas, develops social attitudes for interaction with others and the world. The second group,

Patanjali	**Mindfulness in Action**
Yamas	**Social Attitudes**
Non-violence	Be Compassionate
Truthfulness	Make Words Matter
Non-stealing	Appreciate
Control of sensual pleasures	Be Intentional
Freedom from wanting	Value What Lies Within
Niyamas	**Individual Attitudes**
Cleanliness	Care for Yourself
Contentment	Be Content
Discipline	Take Action
Self-Study	Study
Devotion/Surrender	Share yourself

niyamas, develops individual attitudes towards yourself. Like limbs of a tree, these stages branch out and develop independently while connected to the other limbs and the whole tree.

These attitudes are the foundation of yoga practice and help ground you in a solid practice when your environment might be modeling something different. Combined with a physical practice on the mat, they free an individual from images or thoughts that cloud the mind. On the mat, you practice and experience a different kind of interaction (compassion, for instance), and once felt, you can take that attitude off the mat among friends and family and strangers. Perhaps reading this will motivate you to look into Patanjali's complete book of the *Sutras*.

The Practice Structure

When I teach youth classes, students often ask at the beginning of class for poses to help them relieve back, knee, ankle, elbow, or torn hamstring pain. The sequences of yoga poses in this book do not address a specific injury. Rather, they are sequences to help counteract a particular obstacle with which you might be struggling by altering your attitude. The poses embody the attitude when you keep that particular attitude in mind. You sit slouched, for example, and your body takes on an attitude (a posture) of boredom and lethargy. Similarly, when you stand or sit tall, your body assumes an attitude of strength and readiness.

As mentioned previously, your breath is a good indication of your energy level. If your breath is quiet, you are calm. If you are holding your breath or it's jagged, you are struggling, like those choppy waves. Keep your breath flowing freely for a clearer mirror.

Each of the following chapters will discuss an attitude off the mat and on the mat. After an explanation of the attitude, I offer a breathing practice to center your physical practice. A seated pose will begin each practice. The word *asana* (*a-sana*) means pose or posture, so all the names of yoga poses end in *asana*. My hatha yoga background informs the yoga sequences. You will find a list of poses that you can do individually to feel the pose in that moment or flow through as you become more comfortable with the poses.

Follow the models  through the sequences and read the pose descriptions. As you become more familiar with the poses, the illustrations will guide you through the sequences. You might finish the yoga sequence quickly. If you have more time, try it a second time. Each sequence is different and supports the attitude on which you are working. Keep the attitude in mind as you do the physical sequence in order to experience it while on the mat—and take it off the mat as well. Let's do this.[11]

What Do You Need to Practice Yoga Poses?

1. Just you in a clean space large enough for you to stretch in all directions. A sticky yoga mat is good to keep you from slipping, but the beauty of the practice is that it only takes *you* to do. It's preferable to have space so that you don't bump into things.
2. Avoid eating a big meal shortly before.
3. Comfortable clothes to allow movement.
4. Breathe through your nose, not your mouth, to keep your breath soft. Breathing through your nose slows down and softens your breath for calming movements.

II.2. The Yamas of Patanjali: Social Attitudes

Patanjali lists the yamas—universal principles of how to act in the world—as restrictions ("Don't do this. Don't do that."). I reframe these principles of restriction into actions to better understand what you can do instead of what you shouldn't do. Since you were a child, you've been told and taught not to strike out in anger, and still, there is violence in the world. If you think of these principles as attitudes, you perceive them as ways to actively be in the world, not limiting us but rather guiding us to action that joins us.

Mindfulness off the Mat

1. Be Compassionate: Non-violence (*Ahimsa*)

Instead of restricting your behavior, compassion leads you to act. You don't only have compassion for another, but you also act kindly towards them. Telling someone not to harm others opens the definition of "harm" to a wide interpretation. Harm can include physical, emotional, or mental aggression against others, as well as at yourself. Sometimes you harm consciously, even intentionally, but you can also harm unconsciously, meaning without thinking about it. You can lash out in fear or ignorance or restlessness. And yet, it doesn't necessarily help those seeking ways to act.

Treating others with kindness is an alternative to being harmful. If you practice an attitude of compassion, you stem an aggressive reaction. Your go-to method becomes one of non-judgmental compassion (rather than harm and defense) because you consider the person with whom you are interacting.

For example, Julia walks home every day from the bus stop. She keeps her head down while she walks so that she comes across as unapproachable. One day, she stumbles into Thomas and gets into a verbal fight with him. Since she hadn't been paying attention, Julia can't say for sure who was at fault, but she doesn't like being accused of something. Thomas is irritated that this girl wasn't even watching where she was going. She thinks he was at fault, and he thinks she was at fault. Now both are on the defensive.

Kindness, on the other hand, is attentiveness to an individual. Listen to those around you. You don't necessarily need to do anything extra. You pay attention to the other person. An exchange is taking place, and you can guide it. We think of kindness as "acts of" and compassion as a "feeling," as if you are not kind the rest of the time or cannot act on the feeling. Simone Weil, a French philosopher, living in the early 20th century, writes that when you look another person in the eye, you acknowledge that individual, and that is a simple act of compassion.[12] You allow yourself to look ahead and be present for whoever is there. This helps you encounter that person on your terms.

You don't always receive the response you anticipate when you interact with others. Sometimes people are simply rude. But you can decide how to act and thereby guide the interaction if you are aware.

Some students of yoga are vegetarian. One of the reasons might be that they interpret "non-violence" as not hurting animals and show compassion towards living beings and themselves by eating a diet free of meat protein. Instead of meat, vegetarians seek out alternative proteins, showing kindness to all living things, including themselves.

Your reason for vegetarianism might be for your health or that of the environment, but if you don't pay attention to balancing out your diet with other proteins, you are not showing compassion towards yourself. Or you practice kindness to animals but treat your family or friends rudely. You might not achieve compassion all the time, but when you practice being compassionate, it becomes a mindset.

Do you show yourself compassion? Taking some time to become aware of your actions and words is like shining a light on your behavior. Are you reacting or over-reacting? Check in with yourself, just as you would with a good friend. In this way, the attitude of compassion towards others transfers to actions and thoughts directed at yourself. Can you sit for a moment and listen? Can you forgive your mistakes: the missed opportunity, the bad grade, the rude remark, the hurtful act? Can you accept your body, your thoughts? When you practice being kind to yourself, you can be kind to others. Being compassionate towards yourself and others is a way of being present in the moment. Sometimes you will slip up and act inappropriately; compassion allows you to forgive yourself and move forward.

Practicing Compassion on the Mat

Pay attention to the sensations of your body and your breath while you do the following sequence. Avoid pushing your body into positions that hurt or don't feel "right" for you.

1. Cross Legs. Begin your practice sitting cross-legged with a straight spine and relax your face. Take 3 deep breaths. Draw your attention to your breath. As you breathe in and out, let an incident that has been bothering you fade every time you exhale. With your next inhalation, visualize yourself breathing in your favorite color or your favorite scent. Do this 5-10 times.

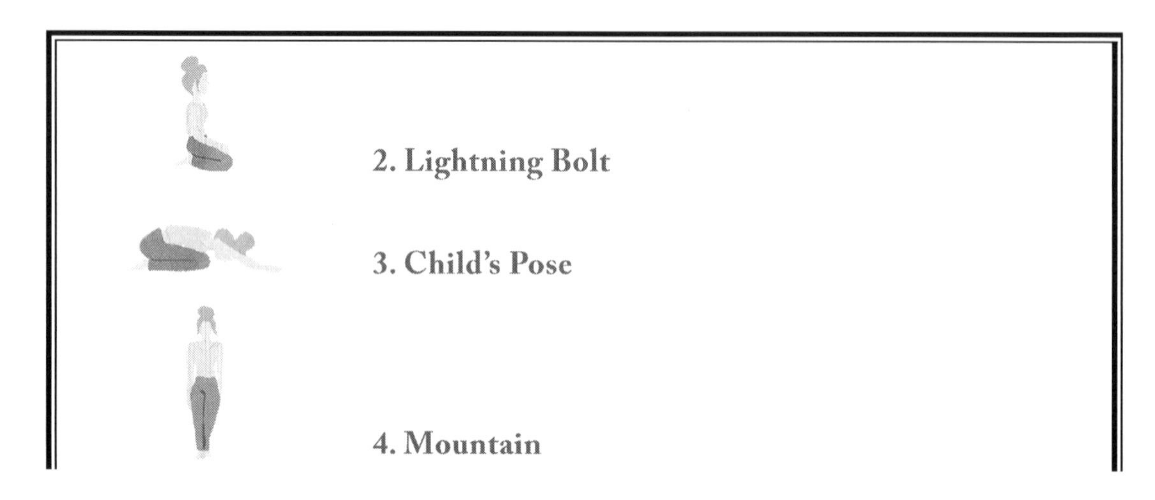

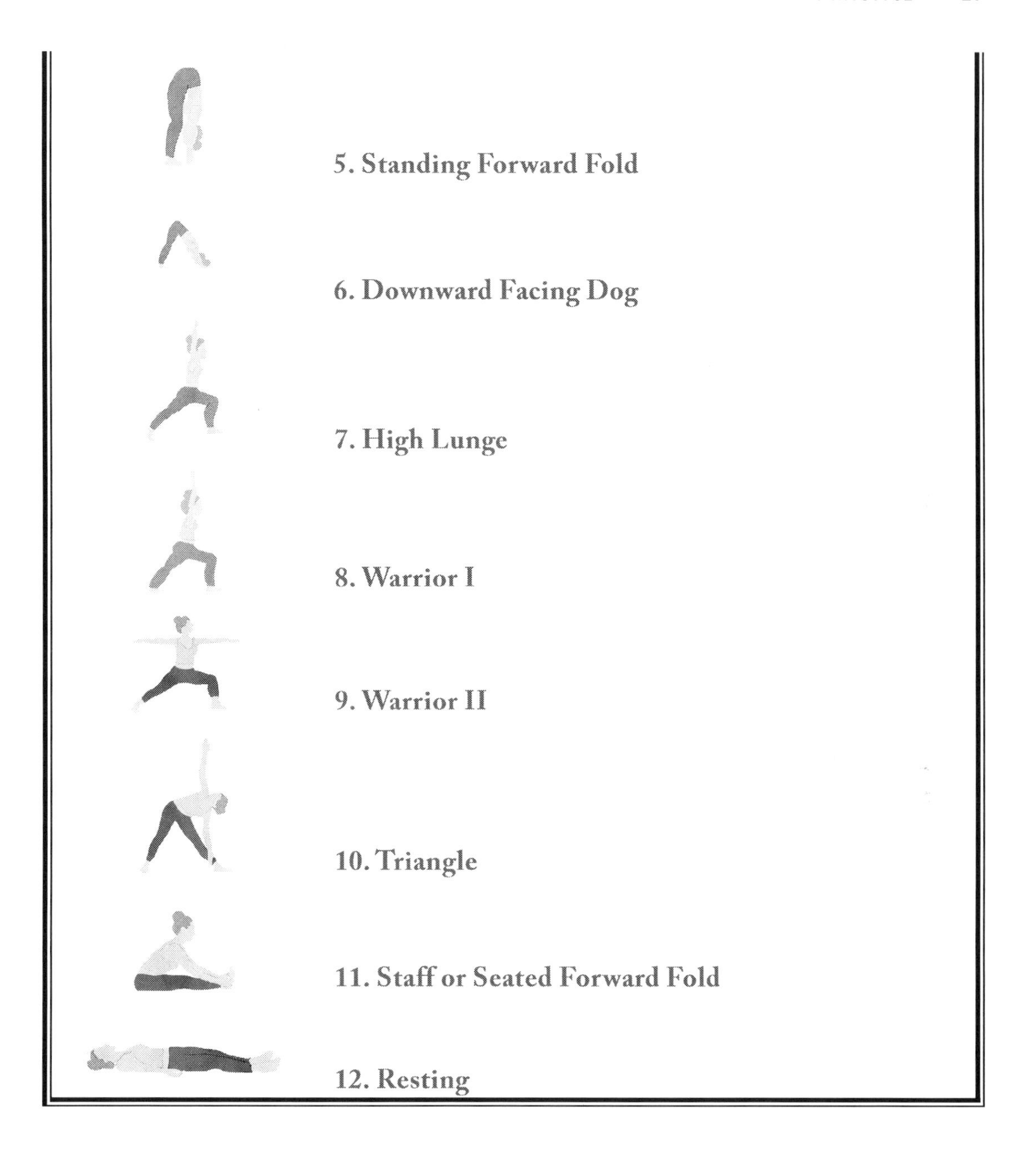
5. Standing Forward Fold
6. Downward Facing Dog
7. High Lunge
8. Warrior I
9. Warrior II
10. Triangle
11. Staff or Seated Forward Fold
12. Resting

Yoga Pose Descriptions

1. **Cross Legs Pose (*Sukhasana*):** Sit with your legs crossed. Lift along your spine through the top of your head to sit tall.
2. **Lightning Bolt Pose (*Vajrasana*):** Kneel and sit back on your heels with your toes pointing directly back. Rest your hands on your thighs.
3. **Child's Pose (*Balasana*):** Kneel and sit back on your heels. Walk your hands forward, so your front body rests on your thighs and your head on the floor. Curl up in a ball or stretch out from your hips to your hands.
4. **Mountain Pose (*Tadasana*):** Pay attention to the weight on your feet and where you feel it. Stand up straighter, as if you were reaching for the sky, reaching towards the sun that brings you energy and vibrancy. As you stand focused on these physical sensations, let all other thoughts become less significant. You could be anywhere, anytime. Stand like this for 1 minute and notice what happens.
5. **Standing Forward Fold Pose (*Uttanasana*):** From Mountain Pose, bend forward at your hips. You might feel like bending your knees. The longer you keep your legs straight, the more you will feel your hamstrings. Keep your legs lifting away from the ground and let your torso sink down. With your hands on the floor or your shins, extend your torso from your hips to your head as straight as if you were standing in Mountain Pose. Then sink down again. Do this a few times before allowing your body to stretch in stillness.
6. **Downward Facing Dog Pose (*Adho Mukha Svanasana*):** From Standing Forward Fold, step your feet back, so your hips are the highest part of your pose. Like a dog, stretch back into your hips and heels and feel what parts of your body lengthen.
7. **High Lunge Pose (*Ashta Chandrasana*):** Step your right foot forward from Downward Dog, and keeping your right knee bent over your right ankle and back heel off the floor, bring yourself upright with your shoulders over your hips. If your balance allows, raise arms overhead. Step back into Downward Dog and change feet.
8. **Warrior I Pose (*Virabhadrasana I*):** Repeat High Lung Pose, this time keeping your back heel on the ground.

9. **Warrior II Pose (*Virabhadrasana II*):** From Mountain Pose, step back into Downward Dog and step forward with your right foot. Keep your right knee bent over your right ankle and draw yourself up so that your shoulders are over your hips. Keep your arms extended out to your sides and turn your face in the direction of your front toes.

10. **Triangle Pose (*Utthita Trikonasana*):** Step one foot between your hands and rise to stand with legs straight and arms extended straight out to the sides. Bend at your hips over your front leg, forming three triangles. Step back into downward dog and change feet.

11. **Staff or Seated Forward Fold Pose (*Paschimottanasana*):** Sit on the floor or a chair with your legs straight out in front of you. If you feel too much discomfort in the stretch, bend your knees, or sit higher and stay here. If you can fold forward, stretch towards your feet.

12. **Resting Pose (*Savasana*):** Lie on your back with your arms and legs straight but relaxed. Close your eyes or keep them open. Let your muscles loose. Draw your attention from the soles of your feet to the crown of your head.

Journaling on Compassion

Write about how you overcame any of the obstacles from Chapter 3 (illness, negative self-talk, doubt, impatience, laziness, anxiety, false self-perception, lack of stamina, self-destructive behavior), showing kindness towards yourself or others.

Mindfulness off the Mat

2. Make Words Matter: Truthfulness (*Satya*)

Being honest and choosing your words helps to build a bond with others. You might not always be able to say what is on your mind, but you have nothing to hide if you don't lie. Noticing what words you use and how you use them is significant.

The words you use create a certain connection to others. When you stretch yourself to use words that embrace, include, and reflect reality to the best of your ability, you show that words matter to you. And it might be uncomfortable to tell the truth.

Sometimes you think a friend or parent is purposely misunderstanding. But are they really? Often, we just pick up expressions we hear others using, such as "You're stupid." Teens are very aware that words can hurt. Nevertheless, you use that word to describe others or yourself even though it doesn't fit. In one instance, you might have forgotten something or given the wrong answer. This does not mean it's permanent. A seemingly harmless word said in a belittling manner is hurtful. A mean word said in jest is still mean.

It's similar to learning a foreign language. When you learn another language, you pay attention to the words and how they're used. Even though you speak your language, learning how to use it to embody the kind attitude within you requires attention. Words can be employed as weapons that hurt. Policies that we draw up in school perpetuate or create a certain environment. If you are connected to the world with all of its complexities, you reflect that with language. You avoid simplifying it to make it one-sided.

On the other hand, you might feel that you are being honest by not putting on a smile or being nice when you're not feeling it. You don't talk when you don't feel like it. Isn't that honesty and being true to yourself? If you live alone, yes. But somewhere along the way, you will interact with others, and if you aren't feeling it, the honest thing to do is say that you aren't.

Another way you make words matter is to avoid putting words into people's mouths. Thinking someone's comment could mean more than what the person said adds words that were not said. Much of today's communication is through images and brief comments. Social media connects the world, and we must interpret those pictures and comments. Being able to communicate quickly and easily is convenient.

However, language and images are only part of communication. Body language, facial expressions, and location offer a context for these. Snippets are easy and fast, but the whole picture matters. So next time you find yourself worrying about the meaning of your friend's comment, ask that person what they meant. The meaning of what someone says does not lie within you. It might feel awkward to ask, but it shows you want to understand your friend. Say what you mean and mean what you say!

This second attitude, "make words matter," links to the first, "be compassionate," for it is easier to avoid harming yourself in the poses if you are honest about how much you can do. After practicing the art of reflecting reality for yourself, it will become second nature to be truthful with others.

Practice on the Mat: Make Words Matter

In doing the poses of yoga, pay attention to what you are doing and how you are doing it. Avoid judging yourself about the *how*. Notice your self-talk and redirect it by focusing on the actions of the poses.

1. Cross Legs Pose. Sit cross-legged and take 3 breaths. Repeat an affirmation to yourself. Think about what you need to hear right now and say that to yourself. You can say things like "I am confident," "I am strong," "I am intelligent," etc. You might slip up and revert to your negative self-talk. Simply exhale, let it fade, and redirect your attention to your affirmation. Do this for 1 minute.

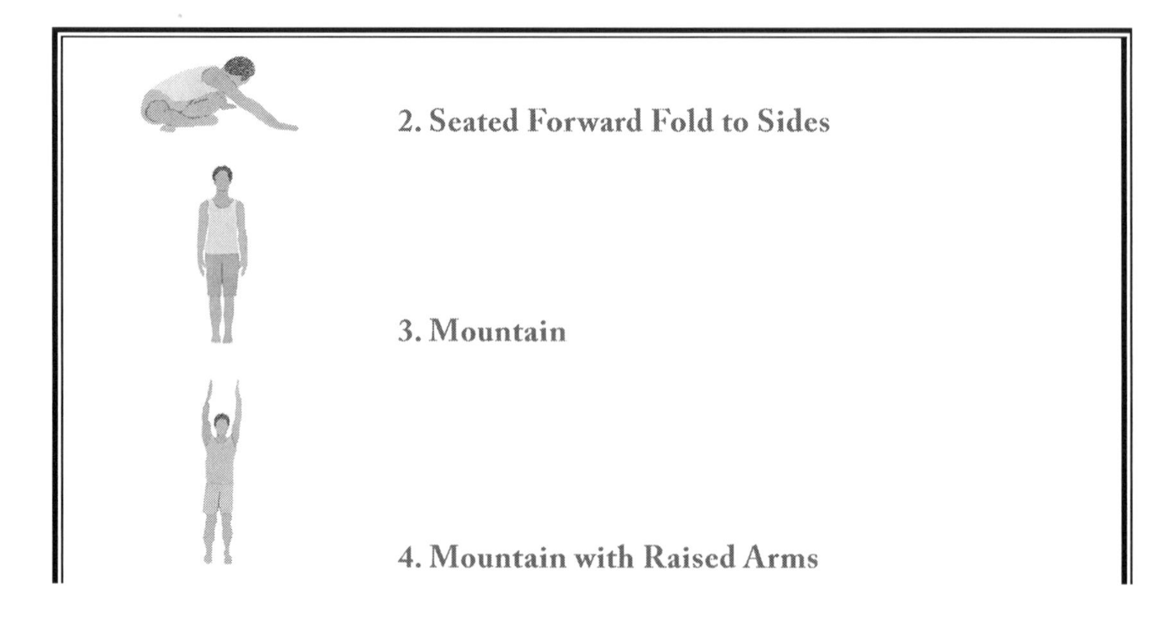

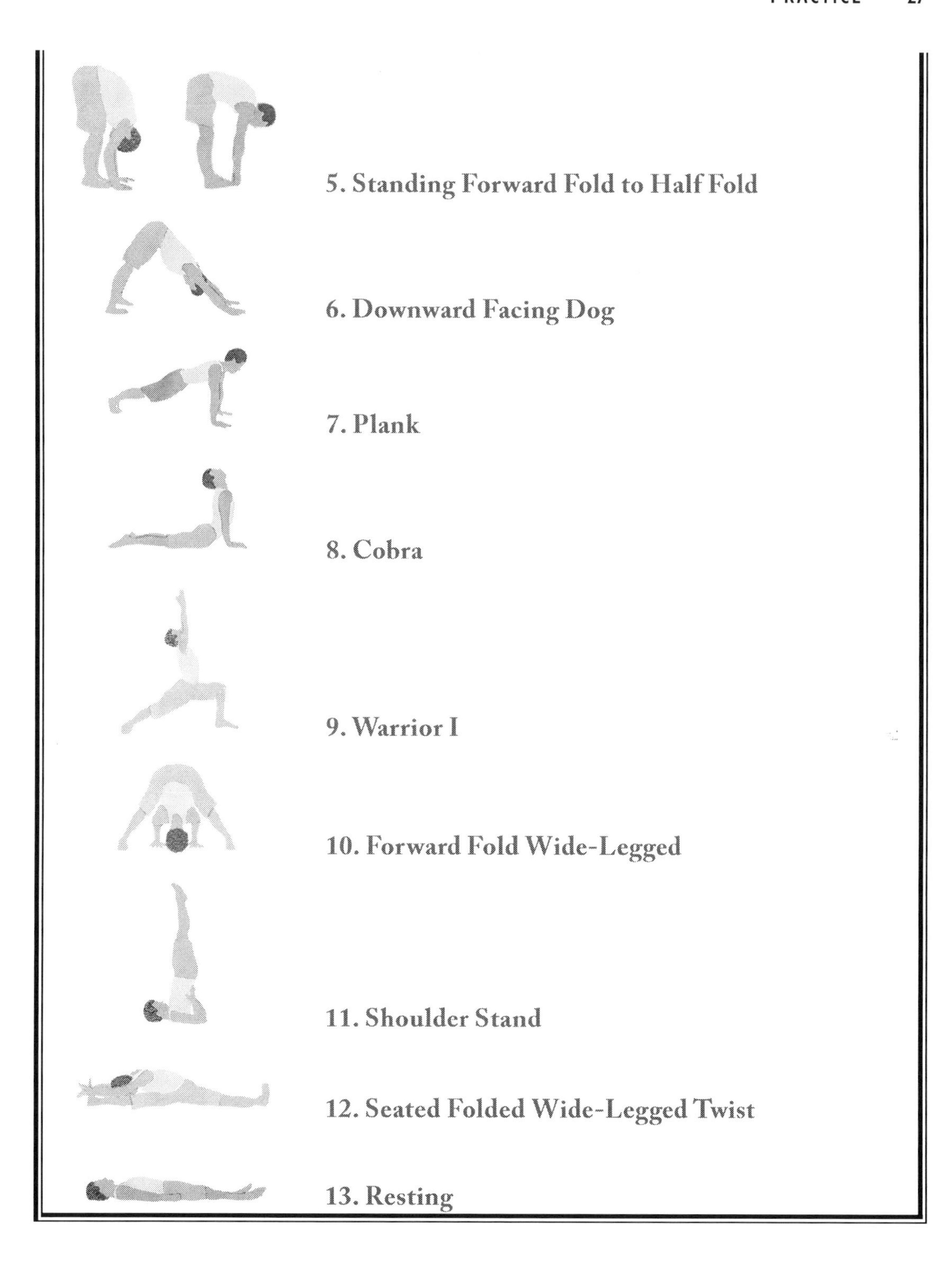
5. Standing Forward Fold to Half Fold
6. Downward Facing Dog
7. Plank
8. Cobra
9. Warrior I
10. Forward Fold Wide-Legged
11. Shoulder Stand
12. Seated Folded Wide-Legged Twist
13. Resting

Yoga Pose Descriptions

1. **Cross Legs Pose (*Sukhasana*):** Sit cross-legged. Feel your feet and your bottom touching the floor. Rest your hands on your legs and lift your chest away from the floor. Notice the sensations of your body without commenting on them.
2. **Forward Seated to Sides Pose (*Adho Mukha Parsva Sukhasana*):** Walk your hands forward on the floor or the seat of a chair so you extend forward, leading with your chest. Exhale and then sink down. Then walk your hands to the right. You might be able to lie on your right leg. Exhale and sink down. Then walk your hands over to the left so that you are in line with your left leg. Exhale and sink down. Resist forcing yourself.
3. **Mountain Pose (*Tadasana*):** Pay attention to the weight on your feet and where you feel it. Stand up straighter, as if you were reaching for the sky, reaching towards the sun that brings you energy and vibrancy. As you stand focused on these physical sensations, report to yourself what you are doing.
4. **Mountain with Raised Arms Pose (*Urdhva Hastasana*):** While standing, draw your arms straight up with your palms facing each other. Avoid changing your standing position to help raise your arms. Just let your arms swing slowly up and lift towards the sky as you press down through the soles of your feet.
5. **Standing Forward Fold to Half Fold Pose (*Uttanasana*):** Bend forward, keeping your back in Mountain Pose for as long as you can with your arms in line with your ears. Then allow yourself to hang. Draw yourself halfway up so that your back is flat, and fold again. To avoid straining your back, come up with a straight back.
6. **Downward Facing Dog Pose (*Adho Mukha Svanasana*):** From Forward Facing Fold, step your feet back, so your hips are the highest part of your pose. Like a dog, stretch from your hands back into your heels, lifting your hips to the ceiling and sinking your heels to the ground.
7. **Plank Pose (*Utthita Chaturanga Dandasana*):** Bring shoulders over wrists. Keep arms straight and step feet back, so your body is in one line from feet to head.

8. **Cobra Pose (*Bhujangasana*):** From plank, lower yourself to the floor and lift your chest up to the ceiling, pressing away from the floor from your legs and hands.

9. **Warrior I Pose (*Virabhadrasana I*):** Facing forward, step your left foot back, placing your entire back foot firmly on the floor. Bend your front knee up to 90 degrees, keeping your front knee over your front ankle. Regain your Mountain with Arms Raised Pose feet and maintaining this pose, extend up through your fingertips. Step forward and switch legs.

10. **Forward Fold Wide-Legged Pose (*Prasarita Padottanasana*):** Step your legs wide apart. Keep your toes facing forward. With hands on your hips, stand tall and then bend forward at your hips, taking your hands with you. Place your hands on the floor or on a chair to keep your back like Mountain Pose. Stretch from your hips to the crown of your head.

11. **Shoulder Stand Pose (*Salamba Sarvangasana*):** Lie on your back and roll your legs up, lifting your back off the floor. Support your back with your hands, and from the tops of your shoulders pressing down to keep your neck off the floor, lift through the soles of your feet so you become vertical.

12. **Seated Folded Wide-Legged Twist Pose (*Parivrtta Upavista Konasana*):** Roll to a seated position from Shoulder Stand. Straighten your legs out in front of you and then widen them in a V. Sit tall from your legs and bottom and revolve to your right, placing your right hand behind you on the floor and your left hand outside your right leg. Lengthen up as you inhale and twist as you exhale. Inhale back to center and change sides.

13. **Resting Pose (*Savasana*):** Lie on your back with your arms and legs straight but relaxed. Close your eyes or keep them open. Let your muscles loose. Rest your attention on your tummy, following its rise and fall as you inhale and exhale.

Journaling on Make Words Matter

Pick a word or phrase you use to describe yourself. Then choose a word you'd like others to use about you. Why did you choose that word?

Mindfulness off the Mat

3. Appreciate: Non-Stealing (*Asteya*)

This is the attitude of appreciating material objects, living beings, and immaterial qualities (the love of others, health, intelligence). When you are satisfied with what you have, you spend less time wanting something else. A desire for someone else's possessions merely deepens your own feeling of dissatisfaction. You might feel that a sibling gets more than you or has it easier than you. By comparing yourself to that person, you set yourself apart. You deny each of your gifts and fail to perceive your unique contribution to your family. At school, you distract the teacher or classmates, and in doing so, take time from all of you. Or you order water at a self-serve restaurant but then fill your cup with soda. These might seem like small infractions. However, all of them create a particular relationship between you and your environment.

When you practice an attitude that your life is full, you don't experience a sense of lack.[13] We take more and more with the internet at our fingertips. We use other people's ideas and words as our own. The boundaries of what is appropriate to do and say to get where we want to be, even at the expense of someone else, are fading. Appreciating what you do have keeps you from craving what you don't have.

You might think this means that you don't strive to improve your situation, but it might show you that, through appreciation, you better understand what you need. Wanting makes us doubt ourselves, generates impatience, contributes to anxiety and misperception, and undermines our self-worth. Others notice your attitude. If you appreciate what is around you, people will gravitate to you. If you attract people to you, you won't need to take from someone what isn't freely given.

Practice on the Mat: Appreciate

As you do the poses, focus on what you can do and avoid the thoughts of what you can't. Feel each part of the pose from your fingers to your toes. Keep your chest lifting upward in each pose as if a string were pulling your chest bone toward the ceiling.

1. Cross Legs. Sit cross-legged. Begin gradually lifting your chest to the ceiling as if it were a balloon floating to the sky, and keep your back straight. Follow your breaths in and out 3 times. Visualize 2--3 things you have that you enjoy. Do this for 1 minute. Check in with how you are feeling right now. Avoid judging your feelings.

2. Child's Pose
3. Cat/Cow
4. Sun Salutation (3 times)
In-Out-In-Out-Hold-
In-Out-In-Out-In-Out
5. Breath with Sun Salutation (3 times)
6. Child's Pose
7. Staff or Seated Forward Fold
8. Resting

Yoga Pose Descriptions

1. **Cross Legs Pose (Sukhasana)**: Sit with your legs crossed. Feel easy steadiness of your seat on whatever you are sitting on. Grow tall along your spine with your strength.
2. **Child's Pose (*Balasana*)**: Kneel with your knees together and sit back on your heels. Walk your hands forward, so the front of your body rests on your thighs and your head on the floor. Extend your arms over your head or along your sides. Rest your hands to your elbows on the floor. Extend your chest away from your knees.
3. **Cat/Cow Pose (*Marjaiasana/Bitilasana*)**: On your hands and knees with your hands under your shoulders and your knees under your hips, round your back away from the floor. This is Cat Pose. As you inhale, move your chin away from your chest and lift your chest to the ceiling, bringing your spine towards your front body. This is Cow Pose. Continue to move from your chest, rounding your back and arching your back as you exhale and inhale 3 cycles.
4. **Sun Salutation (*Surya Namaskar*)**: 12 poses. Stand in **(Mountain)**. Lift your arms over your head **(Raised Arms Pose)** and fold forward **(Forward Fold Pose)**. Place hands on your shins or keep them on the floor if you are touching it. Lift your chest, so your back extends forward and straight **(Half Forward Fold)**. Step back with your right foot and then your left foot, coming into a plank with your arms straight, shoulders over wrists **(Plank Pose)**. Lower yourself onto the floor **(Four Limb Pose)** and lift your chest off the floor, like Cow but with your legs straight **(Cobra Pose)**. Press yourself away from the floor into (**Downward Dog)**. Step your left foot forward and then your right foot forward and extend halfway up **(Half Forward Fold)**. Fold forward towards your feet **(Forward Fold)** and draw yourself upright, lifting your arms high up over your head **(Raised Arms Pose)**. Bring your arms to your sides to stand back into **(Mountain)**.
5. **Breath with Sun Salutation**: Breathe in: arms up over your head. Breathe out: fold forward. Breathe in: lift halfway up. Breathe out: step back into plank. Breathe in: lengthen toward your head and feet in plank. Breathe out: lower yourself onto the floor with legs straight or knees on the floor. Breathe in: lift into Cobra. Breathe out: step back into Dog. Breathe in: step both feet forward and extend into halfway fold. Breathe out: fold into

Forward Fold. Breathe in: draw yourself up with arms. Breathe out: arms out to sides and back down into Mountain (3 times).

6. **Child's Pose (*Balasana*):** Kneel and sit back on your heels. Walk your hands forward, so your front body rests on your thighs and your head on the floor. Curl up in a ball or stretch out from your hips to your hands.
7. **Staff Pose (*Dandasana*) or Seated Forward Fold Pose (*Paschimottanasana*):** Sit on the floor or a chair with your legs straight out in front of you. If you feel too much discomfort in the stretch, bend your knees, or sit higher and stay here. If you can fold forward, stretch towards your feet.
8. **Resting Pose (*Savasana*):** Lie on your back with your arms and legs straight but relaxed. Close your eyes or keep them open. Let your muscles loose. Draw your attention from the soles of your feet to the crown of your head.

Journaling on Appreciate

Describe two aspects of your life for which you are grateful. How could these things help to relieve doubt about yourself or others?

Mindfulness off the Mat

4. Be Intentional: Control of Sensual Pleasure (*Brahmacharya*)

In Patanjali's time, it was seen as essential to deny yourself sensual pleasure in order to gain a higher understanding. Sensual pleasure is any activity using your sense of touch, sight, hearing, taste, and smell that gives you pleasure. Relying on your senses to give you pleasure or to avoid pain is misleading. Pleasure doesn't last, for one. And secondly, if you only rely on one sense, you only have part of the experience.

Practicing an attitude of intentionality, on the other hand, keeps you from seeking out only pleasurable experiences as an escape. To be intentional is to act deliberately. Do you find yourself checking your phone to avoid looking awkward? Have you ever watched a show to procrastinate? Or simply done either for hours? Doing an activity you enjoy is great. However, if you do the activity all the time, you won't get anything else done. This might make you feel stressed about all the other things you need to do. We hear a lot about alcohol, drugs, vaping, and gaming as destructive behaviors, but any activity can be done excessively. If the activity dulls your senses or heightens one sense so you lose track of yourself in the moment, it makes it more difficult for you to choose your next step.

When you are intentional, you lead, instead of having the choice taken from you. By choosing, you put your mind to what you are doing. You slow down to do what needs to get done. How often do you find yourself rushing through activities to finish the tasks only to have your parent or teacher or coach tell you to do it again or fix it because you didn't do it correctly or completely? "Haste makes waste" is a real thing. You waste your energy and time and put others in the position of monitoring you.

Rushing or having your mind on something else puts you and others in danger. When you walk, bike, or drive at the same time you are thinking, reading, or texting, you are oblivious to your surroundings. If you use that time to draw awareness to where you are going and what you are doing, you might feel more refreshed when you arrive because you spent some time with *you*.

Furthermore, things that dull your senses make it impossible to know how you feel about what you are experiencing. It clouds the mirror that unites you to yourself and others in the moment, even though you have a sense that you are not worried about the past or what will come next.

Choosing pleasure is different than using something to distract yourself. Responsibilities can be overwhelming, and it seems easier to play another video game or stream another show or pretty much anything that makes you feel better, rather than be bombarded by those uncomfortable images or sensations. For example,

Isaac takes a bag of chips when he does his homework. Before he knows it, the bag is empty. He has eaten while focusing on his work, perhaps as a reward for sitting still and doing the work. Instead, he could take a break from studying to snack and then return to the work. Consider what you are doing so that you are fully in the moment instead of escaping. You combine compassion, honesty, and intentionality so that ultimately, all those thoughts and feelings you might have been pushing down will not overwhelm you as much when they resurface.

Mindfulness on the Mat: Be Intentional

Go step by step methodically when you practice this next sequence. Keep your mind on where your body is in space. If your hands and feet are on the floor, feel them touching the floor. If your arms are extended, feel them straighten. Describe what you are doing in each pose. Even say to yourself, "I press my feet down," or "I reach my arms away from one another."

1. Cross Legs. Sit cross-legged with your hands resting on your legs or in your lap. Take 3 breaths and then begin to count the length of your next inhalation and exhale to the same count. As you breathe in, count 1,2,3,4. As you breathe out, count 1,2,3,4. If you lose count, it's no problem. Just pick up with your next breath. Do this for 1 minute.

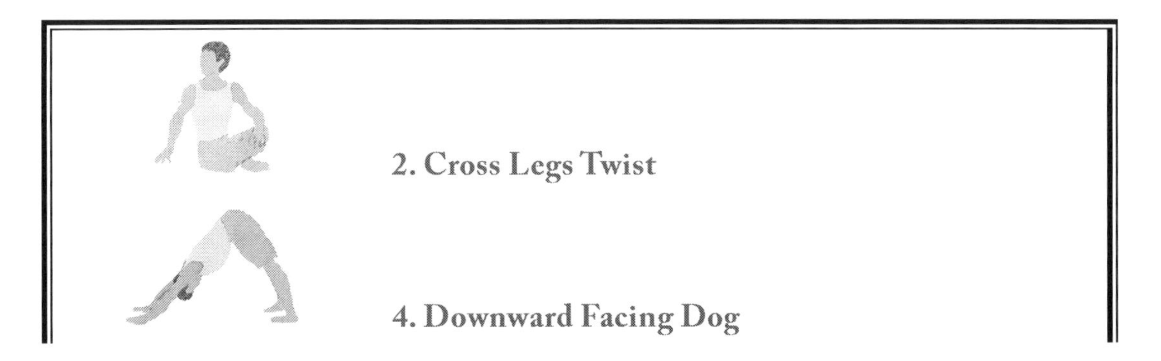

5. Mountain
6. Standing Forward Fold
7. Pyramid
8. Triangle
9. Revolved Triangle
10. Bound Angle
11. Bridge
12. Resting

Yoga Pose Descriptions

1. **Cross Legs Pose (*Sukhasana*):** Change the cross of your legs to sit with your other leg crossed in first. Notice any difference in sensation in your hips, knees, or ankles.
2. **Cross Legs Twist Pose (*Parivrtta Sukhasana*):** Remain seated with legs crossed at your shins. Extend your arms out to the sides and twisting to your right, place your right hand on the floor behind you and your left hand outside your left thigh. Inhale and lift through your head, exhale and twist a bit more to your right. Face forward, extending your arms again, and change sides.
3. **Downward Facing Dog Pose (*Adho Mukha Svanasana*):** From Downward Facing Hero, press your hands, turn your toes under, and lift your hips up, straightening your legs. Step your feet back, so your hips are the highest part of your pose. Like a dog, stretch from your hands back into your heels, lifting your hips to the ceiling and sinking your heels to the ground.
4. **Mountain Pose (*Tadasana*):** Pay attention to the weight on your feet and where you feel it. Stand up straighter, as if you were reaching for the sky, reaching towards the sun that brings you energy and vibrancy. As you stand focused on these physical sensations, report to yourself what you are doing.
5. **Standing Forward Fold Pose (*Uttanasana*):** Bend forward, keeping your back in Mountain for as long as you can with your arms in line with your ears. Then allow yourself to hang. To avoid straining your back, come up with a straight back.
6. **Pyramid Pose (*Parsvottanasana*):** Place your hands on the floor and step your left leg back and straighten both legs so that they resemble a pyramid, your back heel on the floor. Keep your back flat and hands on your hips.
7. **Triangle Pose (*Utthita Trikonasana*):** Step your left foot back, parallel to the back of your mat, and rise to stand with legs straight and arms extended straight out to the sides. Keep your front foot facing toward the front of your mat. Bend to your right at your hips over your front leg, forming three triangles. Step back into Downward Dog and change feet.
8. **Revolved Triangle Pose (*Parivrtta Trikonasana*):** Stand in Mountain. Step back with your left foot. Press your back heel onto the floor. Facing forward, extend your arms out to the sides and revolve to your right. Keep your legs

straight as you stretch over your front leg to place your left hand either inside your front foot or outside your front foot. Swing yourself upright, step forward, and repeat on stepping back with your right foot and twisting to your left.

9. **Child's Pose (*Balasana*)**- Kneel and sit back on your heels. Walk you hands forward so your front body rests on your thighs and your head on the floor. Curl up in a ball or stretch out from your hips to your hands.

10. **Bound Angle Pose (*Baddha Konasana*):** Sit with your knees bent out to the sides, soles of your feet together. Hold onto your feet and sit tall.

11. **Bridge Pose (*Setu Bandha*):** Lie on your back with your knees bent, feet on the floor. With your arms at your sides, press down with your feet and arms simultaneously to lift your hips off the floor. Lift your chest towards the ceiling, arching your back. Keep your buttocks lifting.

12. **Resting Pose (*Savasana*):** Lie on your back with your arms and legs straight but relaxed. Close your eyes or keep them open. Let your muscles loose. Draw your attention from the soles of your feet to the crown of your head.

Journaling on Be Intentional

Write about a time you were impatient to try something, like drive or play a sport. How could being methodical about the steps have helped you do better?

Mindfulness off the Mat

5. Value What Lies Within: Freedom from Greed (*Aparigraha*)

It seems like we already covered this one with appreciate; however, freedom from greed can be understood as an attitude of valuing what lies within. It suggests that you only accumulate what you need, and you do so through your own effort. Think of the times you filled your plate up with food and then only ate part of it. Not only did you take what someone else could have eaten, but the food will now probably be thrown away, which has consequences for you since garbage affects the environment. Why do we often want to have more than we need?

Our society emphasizes ownership and wealth. Many people find it important to be famous or to gain "followers" on social media. This attention shows external value. It is difficult to believe that your worth comes from within. And yet, the actions you take to achieve something—such as grades, friends, "followers," a job, and soon wealth—are a consequence of the effort that comes from you. You didn't simply sit back and watch. These are a result of your interaction with your world. Greed, on the other hand, assumes that you might one day run out of those qualities that led to the accumulation of those things. Like natural resources, yours might peter out.

Your natural resources of strength and suppleness will transform. That is a given. However, if you only accumulate because you believe your resource will run out (buying name-brand clothes) or that acquiring these things shows off your quality for the future (participating in activities in order to get into a certain college or obtain a particular job), you miss experiencing the value of you right now. You place emphasis on the external image. If you only look at the image, you might fail to perceive that your actions or a person's treatment of you (or treatment of others) are hurtful.

When you have a lot of possessions, it's also more challenging to give them a place. Studies have shown that clutter leads to anxiety.[14] So next time you have to straighten up your room, workspace, or around the house, remind yourself that you are also cleaning your mirror by freeing space up in your mind to think more clearly.

You seek comparisons less often when you have clarity about yourself and others. You are now more conscious of life around you and can't help that it influences what you say, wear, and desire. Freeing yourself, even momentarily, from comparing yourself or differentiating yourself externally by what you say, own, and do gives space for your inner qualities. Are you wearing that because you like it or because someone said you should? Are you participating in that club because the theme speaks to you or because you wish to be seen with that crowd? You might feel restrained by adults in your life, but you can begin with these choices (i.e., clothes and actions), within the bounds of your family before you are on your own. There's a difference between comparing external looks and skills, and acceptance of yourself as you are.

Practice on the Mat: Value What's Within

Do this sequence with your attention on how the poses make you feel physically and emotionally. In each pose, inhale and experience the power of your breath, then exhale and release. Avoid comparing your pose to how someone else does it. Keep your breath flowing freely.

1. Cross Legs. Sit cross-legged and turn your attention to each breath in and each breath out. See yourself giving away an object you value (phone, makeup, clothes). Just keep breathing. Notice how you feel imagining yourself without this. If you remain at ease, begin to release more things, anchoring yourself with your breath. Do this for 1 minute.

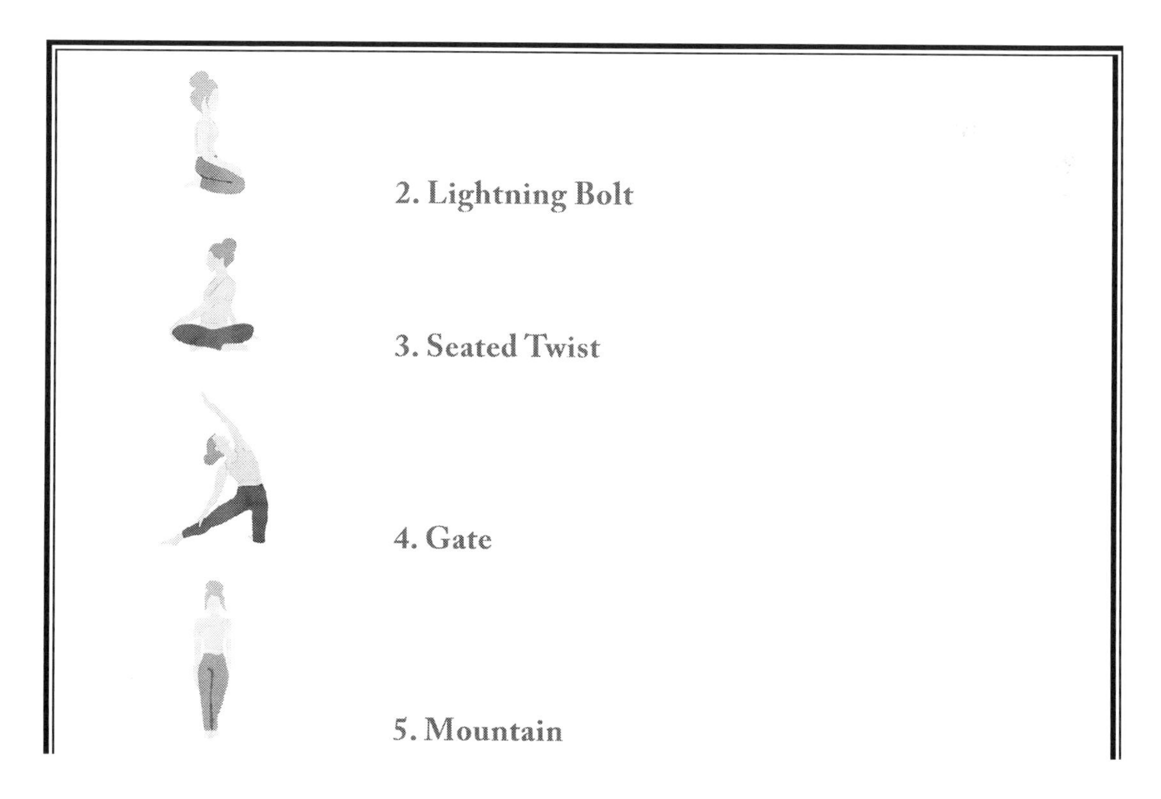

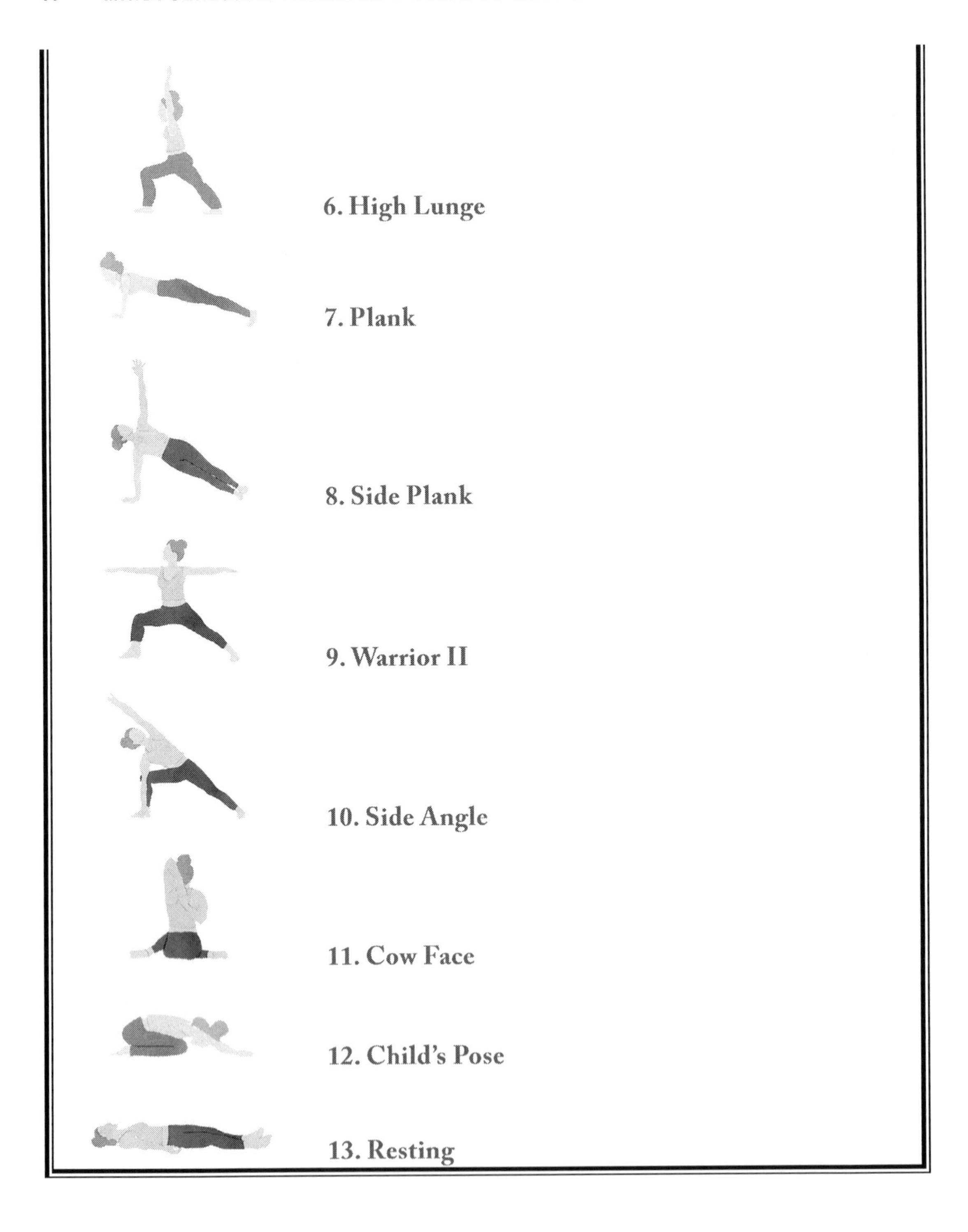
6. High Lunge
7. Plank
8. Side Plank
9. Warrior II
10. Side Angle
11. Cow Face
12. Child's Pose
13. Resting

Yoga Pose Descriptions

1. **Cross Legs Pose (*Sukhasana*):** Sit cross-legged. Feel your feet and your bottom touching the floor. Rest your hands on your legs and let the sides of your body hold you upright like columns.
2. **Lightning Bolt Pose (*Vajrasana*):** Kneel and sit back on your heels with your toes pointing directly back. Rest hands on your thighs and lift from the sides of your body.
3. **Seated Twist Pose (*Bharadvajasana*):** Shift your feet over to the left, so you are sitting on the floor. Place your right hand behind you and your left hand outside your right thigh, and revolve to your right each time your exhale. Keep both sides of your body equally tall as you twist.
4. **Gate Pose (*Parighasana*):** Kneel on your left knee and straighten your right leg out to the right. Extend your arms out to the side's shoulder height and bend over your right leg, placing your right hand on your shin and closing the gate by bringing your left arm over your head. Touch your left hand to your right hand. Change sides.
5. **Mountain Pose (*Tadasana*):** Stand straight with your feet together, arms at your sides. Let the sides of your body hold you upright. Close your eyes and experience what happens to your balance. Draw your attention to your feet on the floor to steady you. Breathe.
6. **High Lunge Pose (*Ashta Chandrasana*):** Step your right foot forward from Downward Dog, and keeping your right knee bent over your right ankle and back heel off the floor, bring yourself upright with your shoulders over your hips. If your balance allows, raise arms overhead. Step back into Downward Dog and change feet.
7. **Plank Pose (*Utthita Chaturanga Dandasana*):** Bring shoulders over wrists. Keep arms straight and step feet back, so your body is in one line from feet to head.
8. **Side Plank Pose (*Vasisthasana*):** Shift your weight onto your right hand and turn onto your right side. Press your right foot and right hand onto the floor while you stretch your left arm and lift your left hip to the ceiling. Return to Plank Pose and change sides.

9. **Warrior II Pose (Virabhadrasana II):** From Mountain Pose, step your left foot back into a lunge. Place your back heel on the floor, toes facing the side edge of the mat. Facing the side of your mat, extend your arms out to the sides, right arm over your right leg. Keep your back leg straight and bend your front knee over your front ankle. Widen your legs if you need more space. Lift the sides of your torso and look over your right hand. Shift your back foot into a lunge and step forward to change sides. Place your hands down if you'd like support.
10. **Side Angle Pose (*Parsvakonasana*):** From Warrior II, extend your right side over your bent right leg and place your right hand on the floor inside your front foot. Stretch your left arm over your left ear and look up to the ceiling under your arm. Stretch your entire left side. Return to Warrior II and change sides as you did in the fifth pose.
11. **Cow Face Pose (*Gomukhasana*):** Sit cross-legged with your right leg in first. Begin to bring your knees towards one another so that your left knee rests over your right, and your feet rest on either side of your hips. Raise your arms over your head. Keep your right arm up and swing your left arm behind your back. Bend your right arm to clasp your hands together at your back. To come out, straighten your arms over your head and straighten your legs in front of you. Change sides.
12. **Child's Pose (*Balasana*):** Kneel and sit back on your heels. Walk your hands forward, so the front of your body rests on your thighs and your head on the floor. Curl up in a ball with your arms at your sides, and hold on to your feet.
13. **Resting Pose (*Savasana*):** Lie on your back with your arms and legs straight but relaxed. Close your eyes or keep them open. Let your muscles loose. Draw your attention to the shift of your tummy as you inhale and exhale.

Journaling on Value What's Within

Eleanor Roosevelt (First Lady of the United States, 1933–1945) once said: "No one can make you feel inferior without your consent." Consider a time you compared yourself to someone else. How could focusing on your own worth have changed that interaction?

II.3. Niyamas: Individual Attitudes

While the previous social attitudes inform how you interact with others and your environment, the individual attitudes offer a personal guide that emphasizes self-care in order to become responsible for yourself. In doing so, you gain the tools to navigate the stressors of your life.

Mindfulness off the Mat

1. Care for Yourself: Cleanliness (*Saucha*)

With an attitude of self-care, you begin to apply your practice specifically to you. You take care of yourself to feel good and prepare yourself to move through your day appropriately. Unexpected things happen, but in the rituals of cleaning and maintaining health, you reinforce bonds to yourself and your environment. Similarly, Patanjali's principle of cleanliness refers to purity, both physical and mental.

What you learned as a child, you begin to do as a teenager. As a young child, you were taught to clean yourself (wash your face, brush your teeth), as well as your surroundings (clean your room, empty the dishwasher). As you grow up, you notice that you feel better when you do. It's a sign that you are taking care of yourself, that you care about yourself. The care you received as a child, you now embody by caring for yourself.

This care extends to more than keeping yourself clean on the outside. It also includes what you take into your body. When you take time to reflect, you notice that some things make you feel unhealthy. If the food is unhealthy for you because of allergies, it makes you sick. But you might also notice that eating loads of junk food or drinking alcohol or vaping makes you feel sick, even though your peers do it.

The same rings true for what you take into your body by viewing and reading. Some people like scary, gory stories. Some people like comedy. Some people prefer action. What you take into your mind is similar to what you take into your body. If it makes you feel unwell physically, emotionally, or mentally, it contributes to the obstacles blocking your perception of yourself.

At the Ramamani Institute in Pune, India, all the students had to rinse their feet before going barefoot into the studio. This ritual appeared established to have clean feet because everyone wears sandals on the unpaved streets, and also to keep the studio floors clean. For the yoga students, it reminds them of this important aspect of yoga: cleanliness of body and mind. Even after my experience in India, I make sure my feet are clean before going barefoot into a studio. Through this ritual,

I become aware of myself by the act of washing my feet, I give myself some time before class, and I connect to all those people doing the same thing in India (or anywhere in the world).

You have other rituals for your life. For instance, Leyla pictures a happy place before she gets out of bed. Doug makes lists of things he has to do. John showers before school because it helps his skin. Sara takes her medication every morning after breakfast, so she doesn't forget. Cameron asks about ingredients in food when he eats out because he's allergic. You will eventually find the routine to manage what is unique for you.

To take care of oneself is perhaps less of a chore than to take care of our surroundings. But your surroundings begin to enlarge as your awareness of yourself expands: your environment begins with your room, your house, your school, your neighborhood, your city. As you learn more about the world and the universe, your environment expands to other countries, the oceans—even space. You are expected now to do more for yourself so that you can eventually enter the world as an independent entity. Taking care of yourself also applies to the environment in which you live. Keep where you live clean. You might drop a wrapper on the ground and not think much of it. But when you care about yourself, that includes how and where you live.

Just as you practiced compassion towards others in the previous section, you now befriend yourself. Often, we don't think twice to help a friend in need or even help strangers in need. And yet, we talk down to ourselves, harm ourselves with dangerous activities, and undermine our successes. Instead, when you befriend yourself, you are mindful of your needs, inside and out. This attention to your needs is the opposite of self-absorption. You pay attention to you, and this kindness gives you the confidence to be truer to yourself. That care reflects in how you act and present yourself. It is a way to clean the mirror that reflects you.

Practice on the Mat: Care for Yourself

This dynamic sequence will help you focus on your muscles and your breath. While you do the poses, consider that each time you use your muscles, you are squeezing and elongating them to refresh yourself. Repeat the sun salutation between standing poses if you like.

1. Cross Legs. Sit cross-legged or in some comfortable position with your hands resting lightly on your legs, and take 3 deep breaths. Draw your attention to each breath in and each breath out. As if you were watching a screen, see each thought you have float by. Once it's gone, let it go. Use this as a way to organize your thoughts. Do this for 1 minute.

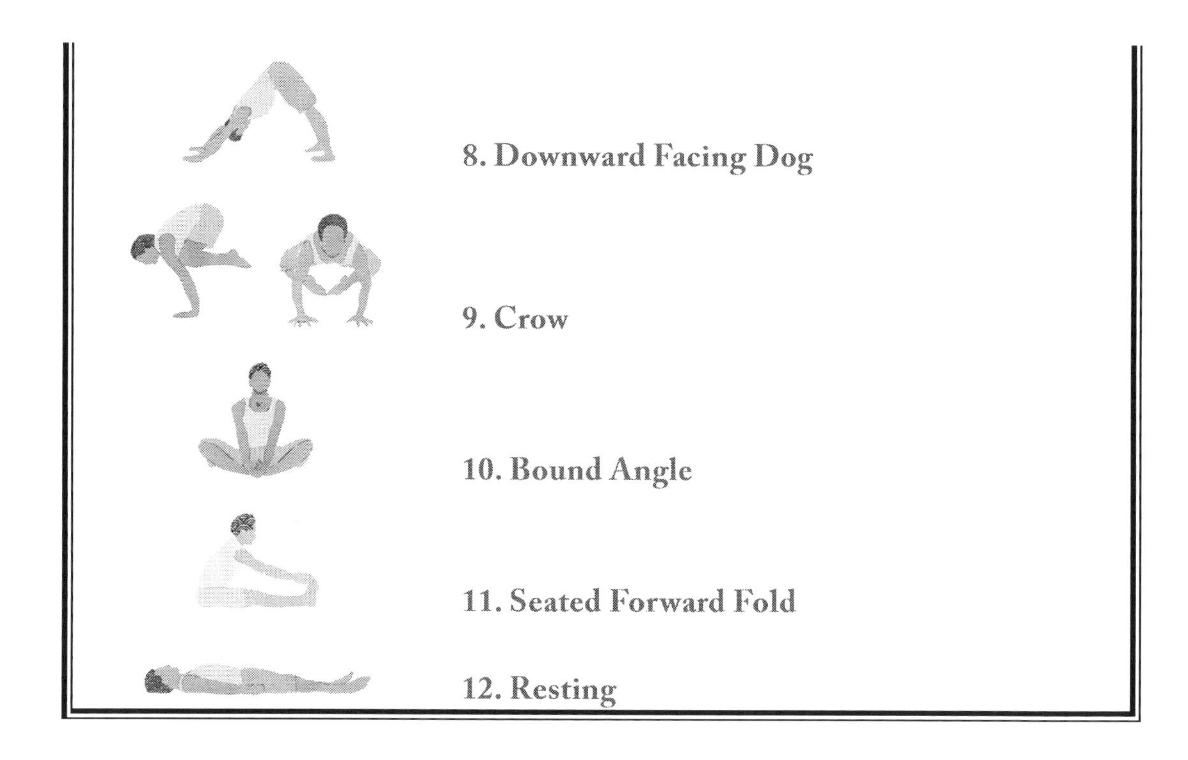

Yoga Pose Descriptions

1. **Cross Legs Pose (*Sukhasana*):** Sit with your legs crossed. Lift along your spine through the top of your head to sit tall.
2. **Child's Pose (*Balasana*):** Kneel and sit back on your heels. Walk your hands forward, so the front of your body rests on your thighs and your head on the floor. Curl up in a ball with your arms at your sides, and hold on to your feet.
3. **Boat Pose (*Navasana*):** Sit with your legs straight out in front of you. Lift your arms straight out in front of you, keeping your back straight. Lean back so that your legs lift off the floor, feet at eye level. Arms remain parallel to the floor and chest lifting. Keep your back as straight as possible by drawing your abdomen in and up.
4. **Sun Salutation (*Surya Namaskar*):** 12 poses. Stand in **(Mountain)**. Lift your arms over your head **(Raised Arms Pose)** and fold forward **(Forward Fold Pose)**. Place hands on your shins or keep them on the floor if you are touching. Lift your chest so that your back extends forward and straight

(Half Forward Fold). Step back with your right foot and then your left foot, coming into a plank with your arms straight, shoulders over wrists **(Plank Pose).** Lower yourself onto the floor **(Four Limb Pose)** and lift your chest off the floor, like Cow but with your legs straight **(Cobra Pose).** Press yourself away from the floor into **(Downward Dog)**. Step your left foot forward and then your right foot forward and extend halfway up **(Half Forward Fold).** Fold forward towards your feet **(Forward Fold)** and draw yourself upright, lifting your arms high up over your head **(Raised Arms Pose)**. Bring your arms to your sides to stand back into **(Mountain)**. (3 times.)

5. **Warrior I Pose (*Virabhadrasana I*):** From Mountain Pose, bend your knees and step back with your left foot. Facing forward, keep your front leg bent and back leg straight. Lift your arms above your head. Bring your arms down and step forward. Change legs.
6. **Warrior II Pose (*Virabhadrasana II*):** From Mountain Pose, step back into Downward Dog and step forward with your right foot. Keep your right knee bent over your right ankle and draw yourself up so that your shoulders are over your hips. Keep your arms extended out to the sides and turn your face in the direction of your front toes.
7. **Warrior III Pose (*Virabhadrasana III*):** From Mountain Pose, shift your weight to your right foot and lift your left leg back as you tip your torso forward, both legs straight. Extend your arms out to the sides, level with your body; over your head, level with your ears; or palms together at your chest. Repeat on the other side.
8. **Downward Facing Dog Pose (*Adho Mukha Svanasana*):** From Forward Fold, step your feet back, so your hips are the highest part of your pose. Like a dog, stretch back into your heels and feel what parts of your body lengthen.
9. **Crow Pose (*Bakasana*):** Squat with your hands shoulder-width apart on the floor, arms inside your legs. Bend your elbows as if you were going to do Four-Limb Plank and lift your feet one at a time to balance yourself on your hands.
10. **Bound Angle Pose (*Baddha Konasana*):** Sit with the soles of your feet together and knees out to the side. Hold on to your feet and lift your chest. Let your legs sink down to the floor.

11. **Seated Forward Fold Pose (*Paschimottanasana*):** Sit on the floor or a chair with your legs straight out in front of you. If you feel too much discomfort in the stretch, bend your knees, or sit higher and stay here. Fold forward any amount to stretch towards your feet. Walk your hands towards your feet.
12. **Resting Pose (*Savasana*):** Lie on your back with your arms and legs straight but relaxed. Close your eyes or keep them open. Let your muscles loose. Draw your attention from the soles of your feet to the crown of your head.

Journaling Care for Yourself

Write about what you do when you are sick. How does it make you feel to miss out when you have to stay home? How might you change your attitude towards yourself next time?

Mindfulness off the Mat

2. Be Content: Contentment (*Santosha*)

You can't make someone else feel contentment; that person has to feel it. According to BKS Iyengar, founder of a style of yoga known as Iyengar Yoga, "contentment is a state of mind."[15] Consequently, no one else can make you feel at ease with yourself. They can do much to aid you in attaining that feeling, but it is your state of mind. You could be in a perfect situation (with friends or someone special, at your favorite place, doing your favorite activity), and if your mind is not peaceful, you are unable to appreciate that perfect situation. Ease is putting forth effort without effort.

Within the word *contentment* (peace) is the noun *content* (substance). Like cleanliness, contentment is related to your content. If your mind or body (your content) is not healthy, supple, and strong, you are often not content. We try to harden the outside by strengthening our bodies so we can feel strong. We wear certain armor in the guise of clothes, accessories, and possibly tattoos. But our bodies are not impervious to the hurt that comes from within, from our mind. So we struggle with our mind. We might dull it, or make it unbeatably knowledgeable. But again, our content keeps poking through or disturbing those boundaries we build up. If you get to know the content of your mind, it doesn't surprise you so much when it pokes through. Likewise, when your body doesn't have to work so hard, you can experience contentment.

Practice on the Mat: Be Content

Do this sequence of poses with your attention on what part of your body you feel working harder than others. Try to distribute the work to other parts of your body so that you feel as if you could stay longer than 3 breaths. This might be challenging, but give yourself some time in the pose. Lotus seems to be a pose for your legs, yet it is the traditional meditation posture for your entire body.

1. Cross Legs. Sit cross-legged or in a comfortable position and take 3 deep breaths. Imagine 3 large cardboard boxes that are labeled thoughts, emotions, and physical sensations. As you draw your attention to your thoughts, emotions, and physical sensations, visualize yourself placing each one in the corresponding box.

2. Sun Salutation (3 times)
3. Child's Pose
4. Bound Angle
5. Seated Wide Legs
6. Half Lotus
7. Lotus

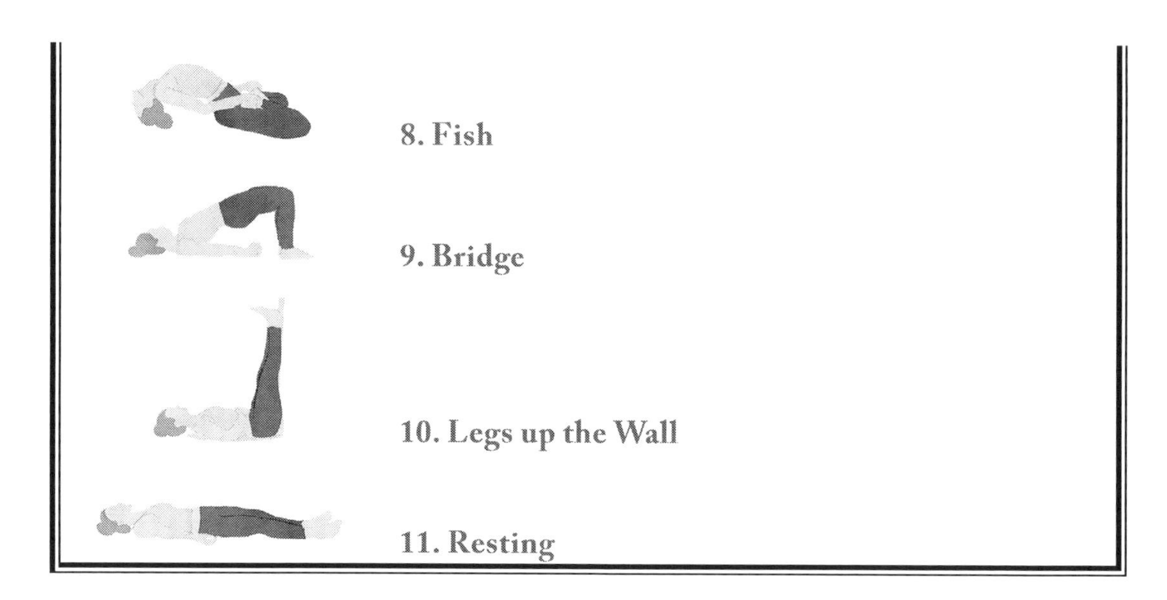

Yoga Pose Descriptions

1. **Cross Legs Pose (*Sukhasana*):** Sit with your legs crossed. Let your body lift as if a string were gently drawing you up through your center while your face remains relaxed.

2. **Sun Salutation (*Surya Namaskar*):** 12 poses. Stand in **(Mountain)**. Lift your arms over your head **(Raised Arms Pose)** and fold forward **(Forward Fold Pose)**. Place hands on your shins or keep them on the floor if you are touching. Lift your chest so that your back extends forward and straight **(Half Forward Fold).** Step back with your right foot and then your left foot, coming into a plank with your arms straight, shoulders over wrists **(Plank Pose).** Lower yourself onto the floor **(Four Limb Pose)** and lift your chest off the floor, like Cow but with your legs straight **(Cobra Pose).** Press yourself away from the floor into (**Downward Dog**). Step your left foot forward and then your right foot forward and extend halfway up **(Half Forward Fold).** Fold forward towards your feet **(Forward Fold)** and draw yourself upright, lifting your arms high up over your head **(Raised Arms Pose)**. Bring your arms to your sides to stand back into **(Mountain)**. (3 times.)

3. **Child's Pose (*Balasana*):** Kneel and sit back on your heels. Walk your hands forward, so your front body rests on your thighs and your head on the floor. Curl up in a ball or stretch out from your hips to your hands.

4. **Bound Angle Pose (*Baddha Konasana*):** Sit with the soles of your feet together and knees out to the side. Hold onto your feet and lift your chest. Let your legs sink down to the floor.

5. **Seated Wide Legs Pose (*Upavista Konasana*):** Sit with your legs straight out in front of you. Then separate your legs into a V shape or slightly wider. Sitting tall, place your hands on your thighs.

6. **Half Lotus Pose (*Ardha Padmasana*):** Sit in Cross Legs and place your bottom foot onto your other thigh. Avoid yanking on your knees. Straighten your legs and change sides.

7. **Lotus Pose (*Padmasana*):** From Seated Wide Legs, bend your right leg and place your right foot onto your left thigh. Bend your left leg and slide your left foot onto your right thigh so that both feet rest on the tops of your thighs. Avoid yanking on your knees and any pain.

8. **Fish Pose (*Matsyendrasana*):** From Lotus and Half Lotus or Cross Legs, roll yourself back onto the floor. Press your upper arms onto the floor, and with the top of your head resting on the floor, lift your chest towards the ceiling.

9. **Bridge Pose (*Setu Bandha*):** Lie on your back with your knees bent, feet on the floor. With your arms at your sides, press down with your feet and your arms simultaneously to lift your hips off the floor. Lift your chest towards the ceiling, arching your back. Keep your bottom lifting.

10. **Legs up the Wall Pose (Viparita Karani):** Lie on your back with your legs up the wall. Reach your heels to the ceiling. Rest your arms at your sides or your hands on your belly. Allow your belly to sink down with each exhalation.

11. **Resting Pose (*Savasana*):** Stretch out on your back, legs hip-width apart, and upper arms a little away from your side chest. Turn your palms up and then let your muscles grow loose. Close your eyes and follow each soft breath enter your nose and go down into your belly, and exit from your belly back through your nose.

Journaling on Be Content

Write about a time you calmed yourself from an uncomfortable situation in which you felt anxious. How could any of the previous meditations or practices help you in this?

Mindfulness off the Mat

3. Take Action: Discipline (*Tapas*)

Discipline. Isn't that what someone else does to us, namely punishment? Actually, discipline is a way to take action. You make sure you get this done and then this and then this. You write down a list of things you need to do today, and you no longer are plagued with those thoughts. You merely check them off. You include time for yourself if you are feeling exhausted or overwhelmed. Consequently, you will feel more content and less anxious about your responsibilities.

Paying attention to what you need to do is another way of connecting to your world. Much of our time is spent complaining, verbally or in our head, about the desire to do something else. In our minds, we play scenarios of situations from the past or possibilities in the future. We think about exercising or the homework we need to do while involved in another activity. Our mind is neither entirely on what we are doing nor on what needs to be done next. Rather than your varying desires struggling against your responsibilities, you acknowledge and make time for all of them—maybe not in one day, but you'll eventually begin to organize yourself within the world you make.

Fortunately, Patanjali believes that with the discipline of consistent practice, you will build stamina, focus, and strength if you did not start out with those. Even better, the result of mindfulness makes doing it worth reminding yourself to practice.

If you'd like to make a change in your behavior, try it in small steps. Place your phone in another room for 30 minutes or one hour when you're distracted by it. With loads of homework on the weekend, do an hour and take a break. Do another hour or two and take a break. Avoid waiting until the last day or moment.

Practice on the Mat: Take Action

Do this same sequence for a week to experience what it feels like to take action. As you grow stronger with the Sun Salutation sequence, you might add it in between the standing poses.

1. Cross Legs. Sit cross-legged or in a comfortable seated position with your hands resting on your legs, and breathe in 3 times. Think of one task you need to accomplish today. Visualize yourself doing the task without leaving out a step. Do this for 1 minute.

2. Child's Pose
3. Sun Salutation (3 times)
4. Chair
5. Warrior I
6. Warrior III
7. Eagle

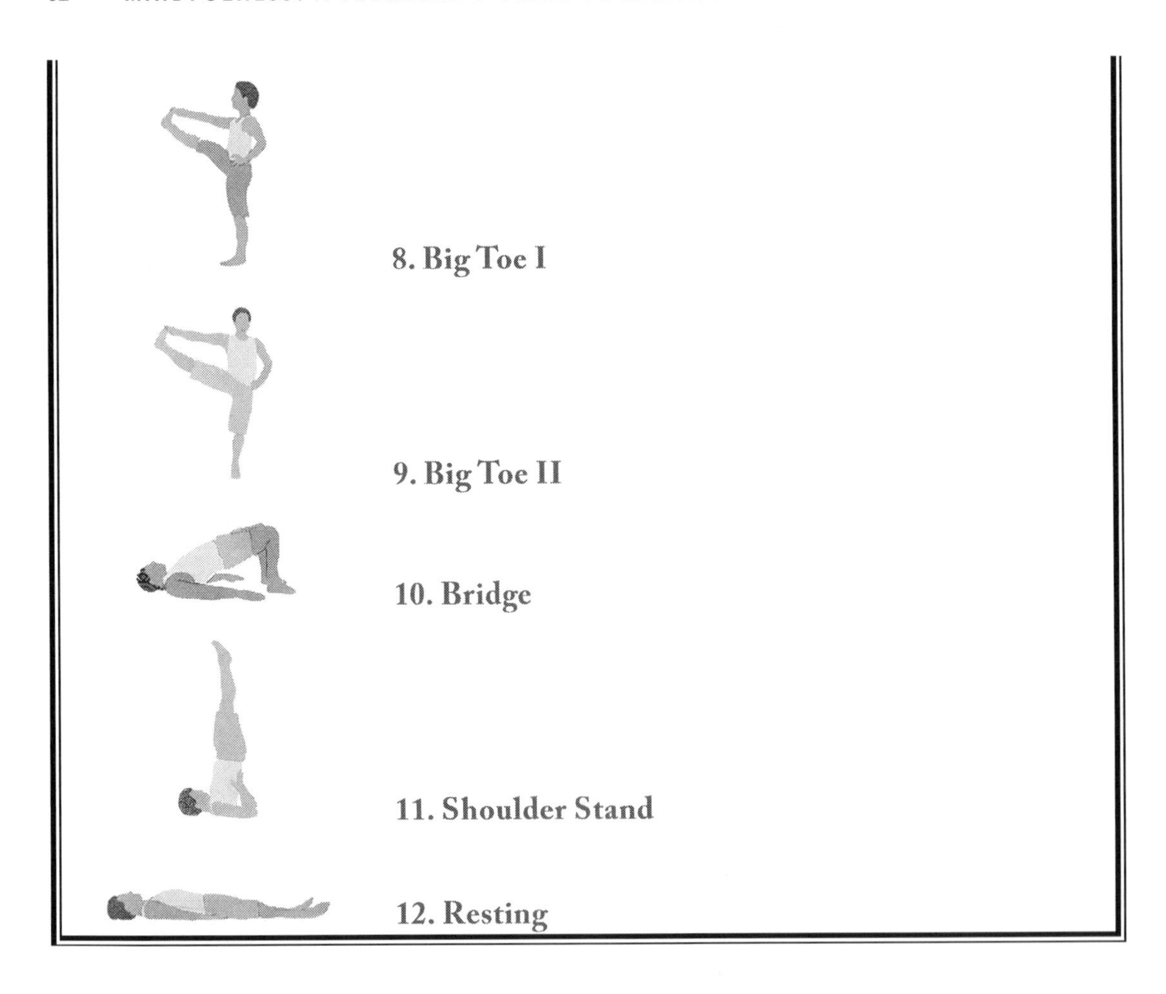

Yoga Pose Descriptions

1. **Cross Legs Pose (*Sukhasana*):** Sit with your legs crossed. Draw your rib-cage up off your waist to create a bit more space. Relax your face.
2. **Child's Pose (*Balasana*):** Curl up on your knees and rest your forehead on the mat. Turn your attention to your breath and feel your back expand as you inhale and sink as you exhale.
3. **Sun Salutation (*Surya Namaskar*):** 12 poses. Stand in **(Mountain)**. Lift your arms over your head **(Raised Arms Pose)** and fold forward **(Forward Fold Pose)**. Place hands on your shins or keep them on the floor if you are touching. Lift your chest so that your back extends forward and straight **(Half Forward Fold).** Step back with your right foot and then your left

foot, coming into a plank with your arms straight, shoulders over wrists **(Plank Pose).** Lower yourself onto the floor **(Four Limb Pose)** and lift your chest off the floor, like Cow but with your legs straight **(Cobra Pose).** Press yourself away from the floor into (**Downward Dog**). Step your left foot forward and then your right foot forward and extend halfway up **(Half Forward Fold).** Fold forward towards your feet **(Forward Fold)** and draw yourself upright, lifting your arms high up over your head **(Raised Arms Pose)**. Bring your arms to your sides to stand back into **(Mountain)**. (3 times.)

4. **Chair Pose (*Ukatasana*):** Stand tall with your legs together and arms at your sides. Bend your knees as if you were going to sit in a chair but press your feet to feel like you are getting ready to stand up. Raise your arms over your head and lift your chest at the same time.
5. **Warrior I Pose (*Virabhadrasana I*):** From Mountain Pose, bend your knees and step back with your left foot. Facing forward, keep your front leg bent and back leg straight. Lift your arms above your head. Bring your arms down and step forward. Change legs.
6. **Warrior III Pose (*Virabhadrasana III*):** From Mountain Pose, shift your weight onto your right foot and lift your left leg back as you tip your torso forward, both legs straight. Extend your arms out to the sides level with your body, over your head level with your ears, or palms together at your chest. Repeat on the other side.
7. **Eagle Pose (*Garundasana*):** Come into Chair Pose. Balancing, cross your right leg over your left leg and hook your right foot around your left calf. Then cross your left arm over your right, bend your arms at the elbows, and align the back of your lower arms together. Bring your fingers to touch the base of your thumb. Change the cross of your legs and arms.
8. **Big Toe I Pose (*Padangustasana I*):** Stand in Mountain. Lift your right leg and hold onto the big toe of your right foot. Standing tall, straighten your right leg out in front of you. Extend your left arm out to the left. Let go and bring your right leg back to Mountain. Change sides.
9. **Big Toe II Pose (*Padangustasana II*):** Stand in Mountain. Lift your right leg and hold onto the big toe of your right foot. Standing tall, bring your right leg out to the right and straighten it. Extend your left arm out to the

left as a counterbalance. Let go and bring your right leg back to Mountain. Change sides.

10. **Bridge Pose (Setu Bandha):** Lie on your back with your knees bent, feet on the floor. With your arms at your sides, press down with your feet and your arms simultaneously to lift your hips off the floor. Lift your chest towards the ceiling, arching your back. Keep your bottom lifting.
11. **Shoulder Stand Pose (*Salamba Sarvangasana*):** Lie on your back and roll your legs up, lifting your back off the floor. Support your back with your hands, so you feel that it's straight, and from the tops of your shoulders pressing down, lift through the soles of your feet. If you feel pressure on your neck, come out of the pose.
12. **Resting Pose (*Savasana*):** Stretch out on your back, legs hip-width apart, and upper arms a little away from your side chest. Turn your palms up and then let your muscles grow loose. Close your eyes and follow each soft breath enter your nose and go down into your belly, and exit from your belly back through your nose.

Journaling on Take Action

Do you give yourself time to do nothing? Write about how you feel after you rest. How could you use this strategy as a tool to help you?

Mindfulness off the Mat

4. Study: Self-Study (*Svadhyaya*)

The practice of studying goes back to the Indian Hindu priests who delved into the meaning of earlier writings. People of faith remind themselves of their beliefs by rereading collections or listening to writings chanted. It keeps it present, and it keeps individuals connected. There is so much input from within and without that clouds your perception. This framework of attitudes, the yamas and niyamas, can begin to fade if you don't remind yourself through practice. When you delve into reading, you also delve into yourself.

Just as you cleanse and strengthen your body, address your mind. Reading books about mindfulness calms and strengthens your mind. We all get caught up in activities and see the world outside ourselves as more important than what is inside. Your inner world is important to you and others because it drives how you interact. As you read in the explanation of self-care, physical and mental well-being affects how you feel and act. If you have a cold or the flu, you feel weak and don't want to deal with anyone or anything.

Our minds can be subtler. You might not realize you are angry, hurt, or stressed until you get in a fight because someone ran into you, or you lost your keys. How do you know if you don't take a moment to access what is going on with you? Wouldn't you do this for a friend? This is another advantage of self-study. Reading books can become a dialogue with yourself to organize those ideas and perspectives you have or that family, teachers, and friends bombard you with.

Just as you stretch your body in yoga poses, this attitude of study nudges you to stretch your mind. This is the idea behind education. Education explains the world but also opens your mind to possibilities. Galileo didn't come up with the idea that the earth revolves around the sun purely on his own. He supported Copernicus's heliocentric theory from years before. We now learn about his theory in school to explain the workings of the universe from scientists, like Neil DeGrasse Tyson, the renowned American astrophysicist, who use this explanation to further explore other aspects of the universe.

In the same way, school offers a foundation for learning, but you must build on that foundation. The stretch of the imagination toward possibilities is what makes us thrive. Denying ourselves this mental stretch toward possibilities (our imagination) cuts us off from ourselves and others.

Practice on the Mat: Study

Imagine yourself as a book. You have a hard binding on the outside that might get bruised and bent from use. You have layers on the inside, like pages layered on top of one another. As you do this sequence, consider your layers: skin, flesh, muscles, bones, organs, spirit (the intangible you).

1. Cross Legs. Sit with your legs crossed or in a comfortable seated position and breathe deeply 3 times. Keep your attention on your breath, redirecting it back anytime your attention wanders away from your breath. Do this for 1 minute.

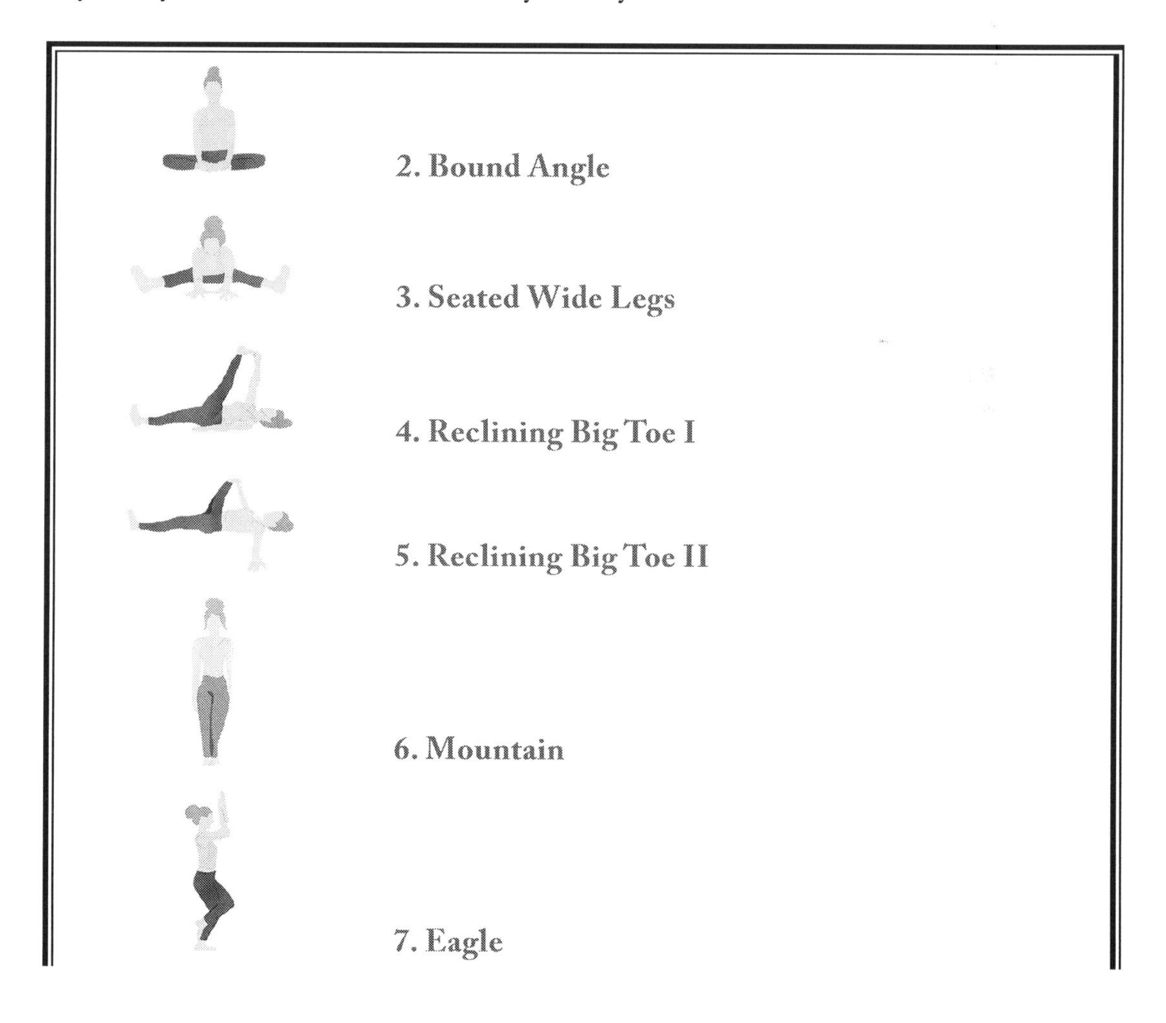

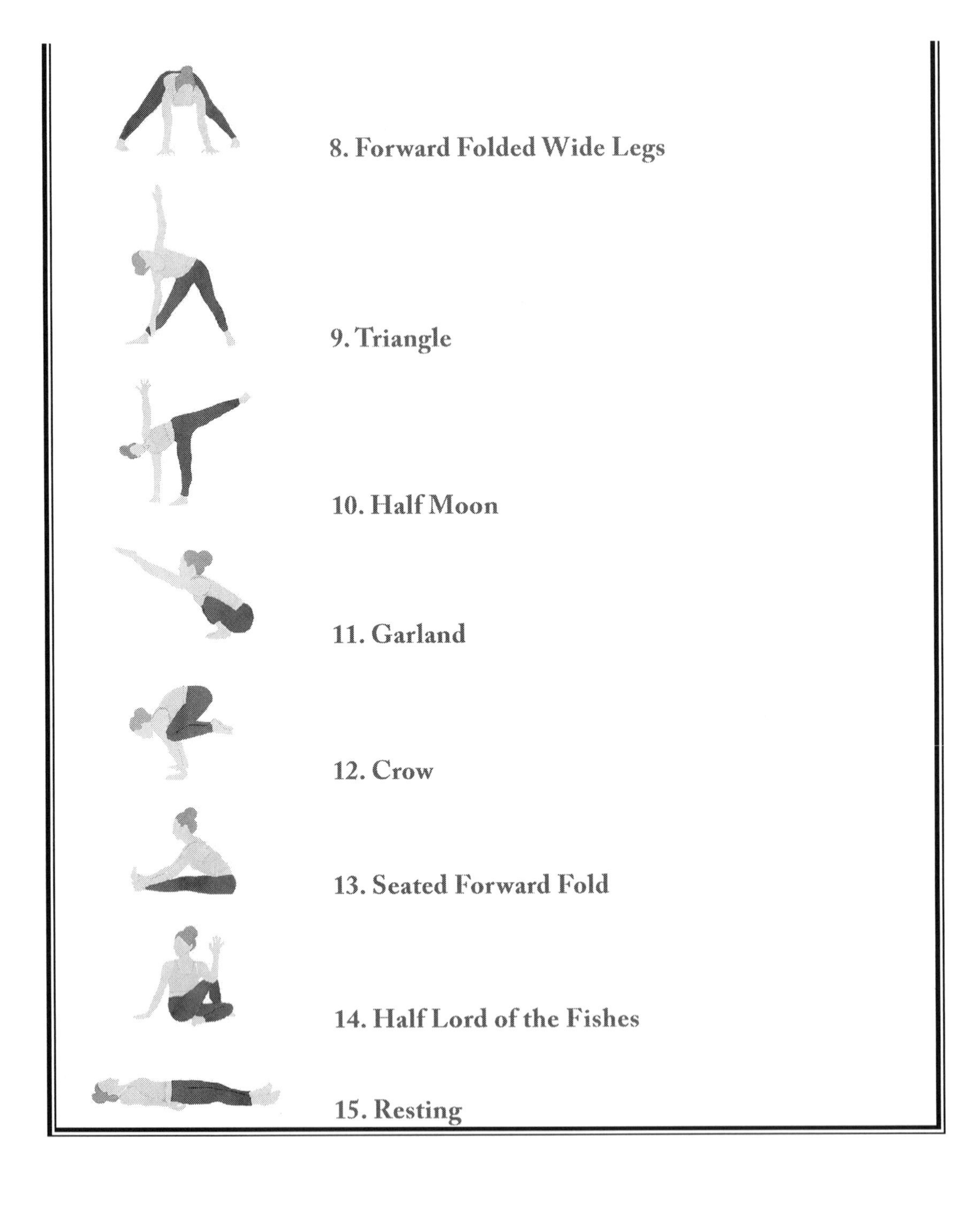
8. Forward Folded Wide Legs
9. Triangle
10. Half Moon
11. Garland
12. Crow
13. Seated Forward Fold
14. Half Lord of the Fishes
15. Resting

Yoga Pose Descriptions

1. **Cross Legs Pose (*Sukhasana*):** Sit tall with your legs crossed. Rest your gaze on the center of your chest, following the shifts of your body with your breath.
2. **Bound Angle Pose (*Baddha Konasana*):** Bring the soles of your feet together. Holding your feet or your ankles, grow tall. Draw your chest away from your legs.
3. **Seated Wide Legs Pose (*Upavista Konasana*):** Sit with your legs straight out in front of you. Then separate your legs into a V shape or slightly wider. Sitting tall, place your hands on your thighs.
4. **Reclining Big Toe I Pose (*Supta Padangustasana I*):** Lie on your back in reclining Mountain Pose. Bring your right knee into your chest. Hold onto your right big toe, and slowly straighten your leg out to your right, keeping your head and back on the floor. Keep your left leg straight on the floor. Change sides.
5. **Reclining Big Toe II Pose (*Supta Padangustasana II*):** Lie on your back in reclining Mountain Pose. Bring your right knee into your chest. Hold onto your right big toe, and slowly straighten your leg out to your right, keeping your head and back on the floor. Keep your left leg straight on the floor. Change sides.
6. **Mountain Pose (*Tadasana*):** Stand tall with your arms at your sides and gently close your eyes. If you feel yourself sway, bring your attention to the soles of your feet. Open your eyes for the remaining time, if it makes you uncomfortable.
7. **Eagle Pose (*Garundasana*):** From Mountain Pose, bend your knees. Extend your arms out to the side, turn your palms up to the ceiling, and cross your left arm over your right in front of you. Bend your elbows and hook your hands together. Bend your knees and wrap your right leg around your left, balancing on your left leg with your right leg supporting it. If you have to put your foot down, just try again.
8. **Forward Folded Wide Legs Pose (*Prasarita Padottanasana*):** Stand in Mountain and step your legs apart about the length of one of your legs. With your knees in line with your toes, facing forward, extend your arms out to the sides, palms forward. Inhale, lift, and as you exhale, fold forward,

placing your hands on the floor. Exhale and bring the front of your body to the back of your body to round your back. Inhale and bring the back of your body to the front of your body, lifting your head and chest. Keep your legs straight. Do this 3 times.

9. **Triangle Pose (*Utthita Trikonasana*):** From Standing Wide Legs Pose, turn your right foot to the right. Press your feet and extend over your right leg. With your right hand on your right shin, reach your left arm to the ceiling and turn your head to look at your left thumb if your neck allows. Bring yourself up, face your feet forward, and change sides.

10. **Half Moon Pose (*Ardha Chandrasana*):** Starting in Triangle Pose, right foot turned out, shift your weight onto your right foot. Bend at your hip and bring your right hand down to the floor to support you. Your left leg remains lifted to the side. Keep your left arm up to the ceiling so that your arms extend away from one another. Come up and do the same on the left side.

11. **Garland Pose (*Malasana*):** Squat with your toes facing forward, heels on the floor if you can. Bring your arms inside your knees and fold to place your hands on the floor. Wrap your arms outside your legs and hold onto the back of your ankles, as if your arms were draping over your legs.

12. **Crow Pose (*Bakasana*):** From Garland Pose, place your hands on the floor shoulder-width apart and bend your elbows. Shift your weight onto your hands and lift your feet off the floor one at a time to balance. You can tip forward onto your face, so practice carefully with a pillow on the floor in front of you.

13. **Seated Forward Fold Pose (*Paschimottanasana*):** Sit on the floor or a chair with your legs straight out in front of you. If you feel too much discomfort in the back of your body, bend your knees or sit higher and stay here. If you can fold forward, stretch towards your feet and hold onto your legs, ankles, or feet.

14. **Half Lord of the Fishes Pose (*Ardha Matsyendrasana*):** Sit with your legs straight out in front of you. Bend your right leg and step your foot outside your left leg. Lean to your left and bend your left foot outside your right hip. Sit evenly on your right and left bottom and lift along your spine. Hug your right knee with your left arm to twist to the right, your right hand

behind you on the floor for support. Straighten your legs out in front of you and cross your left foot over your right leg to twist to the left.

15. **Resting Pose (*Savasana*):** Lie on your back and keep your attention on the relaxed stillness of your body. Imagine your body as a still lake, reflecting a cloudless blue sky.

Journaling on Study

It's not only physical activity that takes stamina to keep up. Sometimes doing academic work can grow tedious. Write about things you enjoy doing or reading about. Describe why those activities take less effort.

Mindfulness off the Mat

5. Share Yourself: Devotion (*Isvara-Pranidhana*)

After practicing these nine attitudes, you might expect that you will attain a goal—health, calmness, determination, focus...something that makes you feel better for following this path. You do experience these qualities, but the next interaction could push you out of this state. Every practice gives you something else more lasting: insight. Patanjali reminds us that through mindfulness, we have gained insight into ourselves and of our connections to other beings and the world. This encourages us to interact more responsibly in life as it continues to change.

Humans can give life and can take life. We can manage life so that we feel like we have everything under control. But there are forces greater than us (nature, divinity) that can rearrange it. Thus, Patanjali drops in the last practice. Devote yourself to something that benefits others, not just yourself. Many schools require a certain amount of service to be done outside of school. Your family might insist that you participate in some service outside the home or for the family, caring for grandparents or younger siblings.

Service is a form of generosity. Offered with love, you give something of yourself back to the community, back to your universe. In doing so, you remind yourself that you are not all that, despite your accomplishments or what you have. Who wants to be reminded of connectedness when you are trying to become an individual? To realize that no matter what you have physically, emotionally, and mentally, whether you believe it's a lot or sometimes a little, you still have a uniqueness that can aid another. It can soothe and empower you to overcome any of the nine obstacles in I.3.

You don't necessarily have to go out of your way. You could help someone avoid a dangerous situation, help with work, spend time doing an activity another enjoys, throw out the garbage. What you do for someone else is a step towards devotion to life. This connects you to others and lifts your spirit. But beware! If you merely fulfill those hours or complain throughout the family outing, you are not mentally present. You are not attentive. Instead, simply offer it up as sharing a part of you.

Practice on the Mat: Share Yourself

While you do the poses, consider how each part of the pose supports and aids the other parts. Link the poses together by moving as smoothly as possible between each one. If you are feeling low energy, support your back. Chest openers are a way to open your heart center. You lift and broaden physically to make space and allow yourself time to be with your fragility. We all have this in common.

1. Cross Legs. Sit comfortably in a chair or cross-legged. Breathe deeply 3 times. Then follow your breath and find your natural pace and rhythm. Just watch your breath as if you were encountering it for the first time. Clear your mind of all preconceptions and expectations.

6. Tree
7. Crescent
8. Warrior II
9. Triangle
10. Locust
11. Bow
12. Downward Facing Dog
13. Camel
14. Child's Pose
15. Resting

Yoga Pose Descriptions

1. **Cross Legs Pose (*Sukhasana*):** Sit with your legs crossed. Lift along your spine through the top of your head to sit tall.
2. **Seated Cross Legs-Interlaced Fingers Pose (*Baddhanguliyasana*):** Sit with your legs crossed. Interlace your fingers with your right thumb in front and turn your palms out to rest the back of your hands on your head. Move your elbows back and raise your interlaced hands to the ceiling. Lift from your bottom to your palms. Bring your hands down and change the interlock of your fingers with left fingers in front.
3. **Reversed Plank Pose (*Purvottanasana*):** Sit with your legs straight out in front of you. Place your hands, fingers facing forward, on the floor, and press through your hands and heels to raise your back body away from the floor, like a plank of wood. (2-3 times.)
4. **Sun Salutation (*Surya Namaskar*):** 12 poses. Stand in **(Mountain)**. Lift your arms over your head **(Raised Arms Pose)** and fold forward **(Forward Fold Pose)**. Place hands on your shins or keep them on the floor if you are touching. Lift your chest so that your back extends forward and straight **(Half Forward Fold).** Step back with your right foot and then your left foot, coming into a plank with your arms straight, shoulders over wrists **(Plank Pose).** Lower yourself onto the floor **(Four Limb Pose)** and lift your chest off the floor, like Cow but with your legs straight **(Cobra Pose).** Press yourself away from the floor into (**Downward Dog)**. Step your left foot forward and then your right foot forward and extend halfway up **(Half Forward Fold).** Fold forward towards your feet **(Forward Fold)** and draw yourself upright, lifting your arms high up over your head **(Raised Arms Pose)**. Bring your arms to your sides to stand back into **(Mountain)**. (3 times.)
5. **Mountain Pose (*Tadasana*):** Stand with your feet together, so you feel the inner edges of your feet. With your feet pressing down, rise through the center of your body to the crown of your head. Let your arms draw your shoulders away from your ears.
6. **Tree Pose (*Vrksasana*):** From Mountain, bend your left knee and place your left foot on your inner right leg above your knee or below your knee. Bring your hands together at your center chest. Maintaining your balance, raise

your arms above your head. Like a tree, gently sway your arms and maintain your balance.

7. **Crescent Pose (*Anjaneyasana*):** From Mountain, bend forward and place your hands on either side of your feet. Step your left foot straight back into a low lunge and place your back knee down. Top of your foot presses down onto the floor or keep your toes turned under. Raise your arms over your head so that your ears line up with your arms. Bring your arms back slightly, lifting your chest, and align your ears with your arms. Form the crescent part of a moon.

8. **Warrior II Pose (*Virabhadrasana II*):** From crescent pose, lower your hands on either side of your front foot and straighten your back leg. Turn your back heel in and press it down on the mat. Sweep your left arm up as you bring your shoulders over your hips. Extend your arms out to the sides, facing left. Keep your front leg bent. Turn your face in the direction of your front toes. Change sides. Warriors are fierce protectors. Consider how you protect.

9. **Triangle Pose (*Utthita Trikonasana*):** From Downward Facing Dog, step your right foot between your hands and rise to stand with legs straight and arms extended straight out to sides. Front foot and knee face front of the mat. Back knee in line with back foot, facing side of the mat. Bend at your hips over your front leg, forming triangles with your arms and legs. Take a moment to feel each triangle. Step back into Downward Dog and change feet.

10. **Locust Pose (*Salabhasana*):** Lower yourself onto your front body with arms straight at your sides, like a prone Mountain. Inhale and lift your head, your chest, your legs, and your arms off the mat. Reach your arms towards your feet. Breathe and feel your back extend in both directions towards your head and feet as your chest lifts away from the floor as if you were going to fly away.

11. **Bow Pose (*Urdhva Dhanurasana*):** On your stomach, reach your arms back and bend your knees to clasp the front of your ankles. As you pull your feet away from your head and up, you'll feel your chest lift and broaden.

12. **Downward Facing Dog Pose (*Adho Mukha Svanasana*):** From your hands and knees, lift your hips and straighten your legs, so your hips are the highest part of your pose. Exhale and lengthen your back.

13. **Camel Pose (*Ustrasana*):** Kneel with knees hip-width apart, shoulders over your hips, arms at your sides. Tops of your feet and knees press down as you lift your chest to the ceiling. Reach your hands to your heels and look up to the ceiling or back if your neck allows. Your chest is the highest point of the pose, and you lift it higher the more you press down with your knees and hands.

14. **Child's Pose (*Balasana*):** Curl up in a ball with your forehead on the floor. Exhale and relax your back. Breathe into your back lungs.

15. **Resting Pose (*Savasana*):** On your back, hug your knees into your chest. Rest the back of your head on the floor. After a few breaths, rest your legs and arms on the floor. If you feel pinching in your back, keep your knees bent, feet on the floor.

Journaling on Share Yourself

Giving of yourself can help you get out of your own mental and physical space. Describe a time you helped someone out or showed a side of yourself you don't usually reveal. Write about the experience.

CHECKING IN

The word *asana* has another meaning. In addition to "posture," *asana* also denotes "seat": the foundation of the pose, your bottom that you sit on, the place from which your posture stems. All of these are personal. When you walk into a classroom, the teacher might tell you, "Find **a** seat." In yoga classes, I tell my students, "Find **your** seat." It's not the mat that makes the practice yoga. It's you.

When we grow up, we think we're becoming more independent. In some respects, we are. However, you are actually becoming more interdependent—no longer so dependent on your family, yet you are learning how to be with yourself, your environment (manmade and natural), and others. You are now being tasked and expected to decide. I hope you might seek out mindfulness as a way toward balance and decision-making. Looking into that mirror can be rough sometimes, but what it reveals guides you.

ENDNOTES

[1] Prashant Iyengar, son of BKS Iyengar at the Ramamani Iyengar Memorial Institute. Pune, India. July, 2009.

[2] BKS Iyengar, *Light on the Yoga Sutras of Patanjali*. Thorsons. San Francisco, California. 1996.

[3] Devdutt Pattanaik, *My GITA*. Rupa Publications. New Delhi. p. 33.

[4] *Understanding the Teen Brain*. Health Encyclopedia. https://www.urmc.rochester.edu/encyclopedia/

[5] Rasmus Birn, *The Amygdala-Prefrontal Cortex Connection is Crucial* (Video). The Raising of America. University of Wisconsin, Madison. https://www.raisingofamerica.org/amygdala-prefrontal-cortex-connection-crucial

[6] *Light on the Yoga Sutras of Patanjali*, I.3.

[7] Ibid, I.30.

[8] "...cells remembered experiences from early in life that then had an effect on gene expression, said Thomas McDade." From an article by Elvia Malagon, "Poverty plays role in DNA structure change study involving Northwestern professor." *Chicago Tribune*. April 7, 2019.

[9] *Light on the Yoga Sutras of Patanjali*, IV.20.

[10] Ibid, I.34–I.39.

[11] "Let's do this" was Jacinda Ardern's, New Zealand Prime Minister (2017-), campaign slogan. It is an inclusive, specific, call to action that mirrors Patanjali's first aphorism of *The Yoga Sutras*: "Now we begin."

[12] Simone Weil, "Attention and Will." *Gravity and Grace*. Translated by Emma Crawford and Mario von der Ruhr. Taylor & Francis e-Library. 2003.

[13] *Living the Sutras*. p. 111.

[14] A study on clutter in *Psychology Today* shows that disorganization can lead to feeling of anxiety, Sherrie Borg Carter, PsyD, "Why Mess Causes Stress, 8 Reasons, 8 Remedies," *Psychology Today*, uhttps://www.psychologytoday.com/us/blog/high-octane-women/201203/why-mess-causes-stress-8-reasons-8-remedies, March 14, 2012.

[15] BKS Iyengar, *Light on Yoga*. p. 37.

REFERENCES

BKS Iyengar, *Light on the Yoga Sutras of Patanjali*. Thorsons. San Francisco, California. 1996

Bryant, Edwin F. *The Yoga Sutras of Patanjali: A New Edition, Translation, and Commentary*. North Point Press. New York. 2009

DiNardo, Kelly and Pearce-Hayden, Amy. *Living the Sutras, A Guide to Yoga Wisdom Beyond the Mat*. Shambhala Publications. Boulder, Colorado. 2018.

Feuerstein, Georg. *The Yoga-Sutra of Patanjali, A New Translation and Commentary*. Inner Traditions International. New York. 1979.

Hayes, Steven C. "Is Self-Compassion More Important Than Self-Esteem?" *Huffpost.com*. February 16, 2015. https://www.huffpost.com/entry/is-selfcompassion-more-im_b_6316320

Jensen, Frances E., MD. The Teenage Brain. Harper. New York. 2015.

MacGregor, Kino. "Why Yoga is a Spiritual Practice." mbgmindfulness.com November 11, 2013. https://www.mindbodygreen.com/0-11386/why-yoga-is-a-spiritual-practice.html

Pattanaik, Devdutt. *My GITA*. Rupa Publications. New Delhi. 2015.

Remski, Matthew. *threads of yoga: a remix of patanjali's sutras, with commentary and reverie.*, October 23, 2012.

"The Spiritual Side of Yoga," DOYOUYOGA.COM. 2018. doyouyoga.com/the-spiritual-side-of-yoga

Weil, Simone. *Gravity and Grace*. Translated by Emma Crawford and Mario von der Ruhr. Taylor & Francis e-Library. 2003.

ACKNOWLEDGMENTS

I am forever grateful to all those who encouraged me in this endeavor.

I am truly grateful to the students, young and youthful, who I've worked with over the years. I have learned so much with you and from your questions and comments. You don't simply accept what I say, but have questioned it and pushed me to clarity. It has truly been through teaching that I've gained the most insight as to how the *Yoga Sutras* of Patanjali bring about well-being. You all brought this book to life.

To those in the yoga community with whom I studied the *Sutras* and who lent me an ear. To those instructors with unparalleled generosity: Gabriel Halpern, who always kept it real with his humor, Suddha Weixler for his insightful training, Mira Binzen for her endless creativity in all things kids, and especially to my early instructors who opened up this world to me. To my friends and family for their patience with my ruminations. To Jersey, who brightens any room with her glow. It was a pleasure working with you. Thank you to the readers who took the time to go through and comment on the stages of this work. A special thank you to Andrea Swank for her editing.

A million thank yous to my favorite teenagers in the world: my daughter Maya and son Ryan. You challenge me every day and bring so much joy to my life. You are my best students and teachers. You are more than I could have ever imagined. And ultimately, to my husband Michael for his unconditional support in whatever I pursue, even when he sometimes doesn't understand what I am doing. He inspires me every day with his discipline and focus that makes any task look effortless.

ABOUT THE AUTHOR

Rhonda Duffaut, PhD, has been interested in identity since middle school when she asked her parents how a person knows which is her authentic self. In graduate school, she studied identity formation and wrote her dissertation as well as many presentations on the subject as it relates to post-war German literature. As an adult, she began yoga classes at an Iyengar Yoga studio outside of State College, Pennsylvania, where she was a professor of German literature, considering a career and an identity shift. She was fortunate to attend classes with the then-president of the Iyengar Yoga National Association of the United States and train at the Iyengar Institute in San Francisco. She has since studied with the Iyengar family in Pune, India; Gabriel Halpern in Chicago; gained her hatha certification with Suddha Weixler; and continues to find support for her youth yoga classes through Mira Binzen (Global Family Yoga). She established her own yoga studio, Yoga Niche, in 2007, offering youth and adult classes, and has steadily built a name for herself as a hatha yoga instructor and meditation guide in Chicago.

Rhonda incorporates over 20 years of teaching and presenting to teenagers into this guide to adulthood through mindfulness. As a lifelong educator, she helps people pursue their journey to answer the key question: How to be yourself, be with yourself, and be in peace with yourself. She has taught and mentored middle and high school students as an English and history teacher and was co-founder and first principal of German International School Chicago. She is sought after to conduct seminars on wellness and has done so for Northwestern University, and lead meditations at high schools, such as DePaul Prep High School. She has been written about in online forums for her work as a meditation guide with Chill Chicago. She looks forward to encouraging more people to be mindful of how they interact in the hopes of generating more peace.

ABOUT THE ILLUSTRATOR

Jersey Benjamin is a current senior at Chicago High School for the Arts. Her artistic endeavors include drawing, painting, photography, and writing. Jersey has developed a growing following by exhibiting her art in numerous shows, participating in contests, and sharing her work on her website (www.jerseybenjamin.com). She has received several awards for her visual arts, sold some of her more well-known pieces of work, and has worked on multiple commissioned art projects over the last years. Her artistic motivation stems from her never-ending desire and need to express herself.

Printed in Great Britain
by Amazon

49140712R00059